CAJUN FOR THE TROOPS

CAJUN FOR THE TROOPS

A. Benton Phillips (SS)

Order this book online at www.trafford.com
or email orders@trafford.com

Most Trafford titles are also available at major online book retailers.

Printed in the United States of America.

ISBN: 978-1-4269-9781-5 (sc)
ISBN: 978-1-4669-0003-5 (e)

Library of Congress Control Number: 2011917760

Trafford rev. 10/04/2011

 www.trafford.com

North America & international
toll-free: 1 888 232 4444 (USA & Canada)
phone: 250 383 6864 ♦ fax: 812 355 4082

INTRODUCTION

The royalties from this book go to the "Wounded Warriors" project for the benefit of our troops at the request of Sergeant Major Elmer Hathaway and his wife Joan with their thanks. (And mine.)

Every American should walk a mile in "combat boots" before getting on their knees and praying for our troops and their families.

If you can't afford a pair of combat boots, prayers don't cost anything. And if you can't walk you don't need feet to pray.

Support our troops.

A.

CAJUN FOR THE TROOPS

BY

Benton Phillips (SS)
aphiliii@yahoo.com

THE KISS OF AN ANGEL

The Navy's newest nuclear submarine, the USS Los Angeles was in San Francisco awaiting further orders. She carried the name of famous warships of yesteryear, when naval battles were fought with wooden ships and iron sailors.

Having had just recently finished her sea trials and found to be sea worthy, she was now going to find out if her purpose was also worthy of the millions of dollars it took to build her.

She was built to be stealth, undetectable by sonar beneath the surface and invisible to radar when running on top. She could sit on the bottom of the ocean at unprecedented depths. They called her the "Diving Belle." And she was fast, too.

The latest electronic gear was in her belly and even had places to put more when it would be invented. She could hear a whale passing gas at a distance of five miles and then tell you what it had for dinner. The purpose of her next voyage was to see if all of the intelligence gathered by all of this sophisticated equipment could be coordinated and translated into something meaningful. Her sole reason for existing was to record a signature, a footprint or even a fingerprint of anything it encountered below the surface or on top.

In San Diego Commander Angela Morrell was sitting opposite Admiral Brown being briefed on the mission of the Los Angeles. She was a beautiful woman in her mid 40s. She had brown hair and brown eyes, bright brown eyes that sometimes looked almost yellow if the sunlight hit them just right. Her face left nothing to be desired; the skin looked like your hand would disappear in the glow if you touched it. If an artist could paint the portrait of an angel, it would look just like the commander. She appeared to be in her mid to late 20s, had a smile that would melt a snowman and a walk that wasn't a walk, it was so smooth that you would think she was on skates. She seemed to float to her destination with almost a hint of a waltz. You could swear that you hear the music.

"Angela, I have known you for over 20 years, I was at your wedding, was there when your son was born and at the funeral when your husband died, so what I am about to tell you may hurt your feelings but I think it's best for you to know what's on my mind," said Admiral Brown.

"Take your best shot, sir, there are no secrets between us. I have the greatest respect for your opinions and judgment," replied Angela.

"You were not my first choice for the captain of the Los Angeles; not that there is anything in your records to suggest that you're not the best choice. On the contrary, your record is perfect, too perfect. I have never seen higher ratings in all my years in the navy.

"Here's my problem. You know the book backwards and forwards and apply it at all times. Never once in your entire service is there any indication that you did anything that was not by the book. The book is written to be followed, it is more than guidelines, but there are times when the book doesn't cover a situation. It is written to eliminate human error but humans wrote it. Remember last year when you sent in a correction to the text of a new regulation, it was corrected, but Washington wanted to know to whom they owed the dubious honor of 'Overseer of Publications'.

"Your looks, intelligence and demeanor lead people to believe that you think you are better than anyone else. I know you don't feel that way and maybe deep down nobody else thinks you do either, but it is a feeling that's hard to shake. So if you are going to make this assignment work, you are going to have to let your crew know that you don't consider yourself as some kind of goddess. I don't know what to suggest, wear lipstick on your nose or put your shoes on the wrong feet, do something to let them know you are part of their lives." The admiral said this last sentence with half a smile on his face, but Angela could tell he was earnestly trying to help her. He had always seemed to be a part of her family.

"I have sometimes had the feeling there was a gap between the crew and myself, but thought it nothing more than respect for a disciplined officer. I will make an effort to change their attitude without losing their respect. I'll have to do a lot of thinking and praying about it. I will certainly do whatever is necessary to make this a successful voyage," said Angela.

"I am sure you will, and Mrs. Brown and I will be praying for you, also. I just wanted to make you aware of my feelings and let you know that your future in this program depends on this voyage. Now let's get down to the business at hand.

"You will proceed to Pearl and along the way you will sign every ship that passes and every third day you will send the information back to us. I use the word sign because we want every bit of information you can glean from your equipment, even down to the color of the captain's drawers if you can get it. After two days in Pearl you will continue on to Okinawa, in route your assignment will be the same as before.

"In the safe on the boat you will find sealed orders. These are not to be opened unless you receive word saying to do so. They are contingency orders.

"Let me stress again the importance of this trip to your career. Now here are your written orders and you will get more details downstairs in the briefing room," said the admiral, standing up and leading her to the door.

"Thank you so much for the heads up and I won't disappoint you, and I'll do a little praying of my own, I guess," she said and left the room.

The Captain called the Exec to her quarters. When he stuck his head in the door she said, "Make preparations for getting underway, go through the checklist twice, no slip-ups. Scrub half of the drills we have scheduled, the Admiral feels the crew needs the rest. I guess he is right, because I am so tired from these sea trials, I don't have to imagine how they feel. Let me know when the preparations are complete."

"Aye, aye, Captain," and he left.

Seaman Sean O'Riley was standing topside deck watch talking with the duty officer when the Chief came aboard. "Chief Warrant Officer Michael, Archie A. reporting for duty. Request permission to come aboard, sir?"

"Permission granted, come aboard, Mr. Michaels," said Lieutenant Fagan. "You're just in time Chief, we get underway in four hours."

"That's Michael without the 's', sir. I was detained at the gate. They said the same thing about my name, but it got all straightened out eventually. Anyway, here I am and ready to get away from those clowns at the gate who insisted that I have to have an 's' at the end of my name before they let me in the gate. It's an understandable mistake.

"Security is tight around here and I can understand why it should be and my name is sometimes confusing. Security is one thing, stupidity is another, and arguing with a man about how to spell his own name doesn't come under the heading of security.

"They finally got it straight, I think they called my mom and dad," the warrant officer said. He had a big smile on his face. "But what's in a name?"

"Wait up here for a few minutes, and I'll get the yeoman to check you in," the lieutenant said and took the chief's papers below.

After a brief interval they heard a voice, "Get logged in topside and come on down, Sir."

They were well out to sea when the diving alarm sounded and as soon as everything settled down to a normal enhanced alert the captain sent for Mr. Michael.

"You wanted to see me, Captain?" asked Mr. Michael.

"Yes, please have a seat. I saw you when they were testing the reactor at the shipyard. You were in charge of installing the power plant, were you not?"

"Yes Ma'am, I was and that's why I was assigned to this voyage. In the event that there are any questions about anything, operating procedures, routine maintenance, log entries or just anything, I am to be the source of information, the fountain of knowledge so to speak. It was the personal desire of Admiral Brown that I make this trip and nobody says no to him. So you are stuck with me for this trip." He had a big smile on his face. He always had a big smile on his face.

"Aha! Now that makes sense. I was wondering why we got such short notice of your orders. I should have known the admiral would find a way to hedge his bet. He is a rascal, but you gotta love him," the captain said. "I see here in your file that you are the foremost authority on reactors in submarines. How is it that you are not out in civilian life making the big bucks?"

"Some people like big bucks and others like a life of order. My big bucks are a life of order. I'll get the big bucks everyday. I have a boss that's outta this world and I only deal with the best people."

After a few more questions and answers the meeting was over.

The trip to Pearl had been more than enough to justify the existence of the Los Angeles. After a brief stay in port, which was marred only by a fistfight that broke out in a bar when one of the crew yelled out "The best Marine is a submarine", the boat was on her way to Okinawa doing her thing.

Ten days into the trip the message came to open the orders that were in the safe. The captain called the exec to the wardroom to discuss the orders.

The North Koreans

had finally built a ballistic missile nukie sub and it was supposed to be stealth. In seven days they would begin the sea trials. The Los Angeles was to lay on the bottom off the coast and get all the information needed to identify and track that submarine.

"Get me a course to this spot here," she said, pointing to an x on the map, "and this time we get the color of the captain's shorts." She didn't explain her add-on.

"Aye, Aye Captain," the Exec said and left.

She sat alone, said a brief prayer, closed her eyes and just meditated. The information from this mission alone would pay for the cost of the boat. Not many ships can say that. "Mark my bill paid," sounded good.

After four days of sitting on the bottom near the entrance of the bay, no more information could be gotten without shadowing the object of interest.

"Take her up to stealth depth, silent running and keep the maximum distance between us," the captain said.

"Captain, the reactor shut down!" Came an excited reply from the speaker.

"Take it easy and have Mr. Michael investigate; give him whatever he needs," the captain replied in a cool voice.

After some time Mr. Michael reported, "There is no malfunction in any of the circuits; we have checked everything three times using different techs on a different circuit each time. No dirt, no water, not even a sneeze, nothing. The problem is in the reactor. I can't imagine what it could be, but it is the only place we haven't checked."

"Okay, let's go through it one more time, I am not going to give up that easy. "Find me an answer, mister, we don't have much time left," the captain said in a voice that was unmistakably an order, but had just a hint of begging to it.

"Aye, aye Captain," said Mr. Michael and got right to it.

A short time later Mr. Michael said, "Captain, we have done it twice more and the results are the same. I'm going to tell you something you will neither like, nor will you be inclined to believe. I hardly believe it myself, but there is no other option left to us. We'll have to visually inspect the reactor area until we find a fault. I'll need two people beside myself and one of the two has to be the strongest man on the boat. I don't know what we'll find, if anything, but I want someone stronger than I am to be with me. The other person has to have technical knowledge and a thorough knowledge of the boat and has to be able to handle the communications."

"You're asking too much for an if that's just an if. There has to be an alternative," the captain said. She was still cool, but had melted a little.

"No Ma'am, there isn't, and as you pointed out, time is running out."

"Okay, get Seaman O'Riley up here and get the protective clothing ready," she ordered. Then she turned to the Exec and said, "I am going in with Mr. Michael and Seaman O'Riley. Once we go in, you will have command of the ship."

"That's not according to regs, Captain, you can't do that. You have to appoint someone to go with Mr. Michael," the Exec said.

"It isn't open for debate, Mister, enter it into the log," she said and turned to Seaman O'Riley. "Did Mr. Michael explain everything?"

"Yes, Captain, and I'm ready but can I ask you something?"

"Sure go ahead."

"Ma'am this is really dangerous and we probably won't get out of this alive, but if we do, the least we can hope for is radiation burn and, Ma'am, you are so beautiful."

"Only a sailor would think of something like that at a time like this," she thought. "Thank you, but that's enough of that. You know my son is your age and he's at West Point. You remind me of him and I would like to think he's as brave as you," she said and then did something that was totally against regs. She leaned over and gave him a kiss on the cheek; for good luck she told him.

They were suited up and ready to go in when the reactor came back on line just as suddenly as it had gone out.

There was no screaming and yelling; no jumping for joy, no high fives, there was nothing but total silence throughout the boat. Seaman O'Riley was the first to speak, "Captain I must not be as brave as you think, this scares me."

"Somehow or another I get the feeling that you are not alone. I don't know what just occurred, but take her up and let's get out of here." The cool was back, full force.

The next night Mr. Michael met with the captain in the wardroom. "Captain, the way I figure it, you owe me a favor and I'd like to collect it now," he said.

"You're probably right, but tell me the favor before I decide if you are entitled to it."

"I need to be topside for a short time, can we surface for a while? It's dark and we need to send messages anyway. There's nothing for a hundred miles around. I really need this." Mr. Michael didn't have his usual smile.

"That's an excellent idea, I need the air also and for some strange reason I want to see the outside world right now." She grabbed her binoculars and followed him out.

On the surface it was a clear night, stars were out and a cool breeze was blowing. The sea was smooth and Mr. Michael was right about nothing being around for a hundred miles.

"Captain, another favor if you will. I need to speak to you alone for about five minutes," Mr. Michael said.

"You have me going against every reg in the book, but you know a friend of mine said that sometimes the book is only a book. I wonder what he is going to say when I tell him about all this. Clear the bridge." It was a loud commanding voice.

"Now that we are alone, can you say 'this is a drill, this is a drill,'" it was a statement not a question. "The crew will not remember me, but you'll never forget me," and he leaned over and kissed her cheek. "You see, I'm Michael the arch angel.

"Your prayers for the crew were heard. You asked for guidance to be able to unite the crew so that they would be proud to serve under you. He floated up from the deck and hovered over the side. Nobody ever forgets being kissed by an angel and remember, this is a drill, this is a drill," he said and plunged into the ocean.

Without thinking she said, "Man overboard, man overboard. Port side."

The lookouts came to the bridge immediately. Seaman O'Riley was first one up.

"Who's overboard Captain?" he asked.

"Your hero, Mr. Michael," she answered.

"I don't know any Mr. Michael, Captain, and Ma'am you're my hero. In fact you're a hero to the entire crew. And Captain, I'll never forget that I was kissed by an angel. That gave me courage. Thank you."

Being swift to assess a situation, she turned and gave the word, "This is a drill, this is a drill."

"Captain . . . Captain, wake up. We're having a fire drill." It was the Exec.

"I must've fallen asleep, secure from all drills today. Are we ready to get underway?" she asked. Then thought about how real that dream seemed.

"Almost Captain, and there's a Chief Warrant Officer Michael topside with orders from Admiral Brown," the Exec replied. "Topside has been calling you for about five minutes."

"That's got to be Michael without the 's'," she said.

"That's right Captain, that's exactly what he said," the Exec said, and then added, "How'd you know?"

"When you've been captain for as long as I have, you'll just know these things," she had a smile as big as a slice of watermelon. "Send him down."

"Well, I just can't wait until I've been in command for five whole months," he said matching her smile. He turned and headed topside.

"So far the trip has been exactly as in the dream. I wonder if knowing the future will change it. The fistfight in Pearl, the contingency orders and now we're on the bottom collecting data again. Everything like in the dream." She was writing in her personal journal. "Now it's time to get off the bottom. Let's see what happens next."

She went into the control room and said, "Get her off the bottom, we're getting underway."

"Aye, aye, Captain," came the reply.

"Captain, we've lost power, the reactor shut down," came a voice over the speaker. It was almost a panicky voice.

"Okay, everyone keep calm. I know this has never happened before, but believe me it will be resolved." The captain's voice was cool. "Go over every circuit at least three times." She knew the results, but was trained to cover every aspect, just in case.

She knew exactly what she was going to do. How could this be?

The dream was true to form, except this time she told Mr. Michael to wait in her quarters. She suited up with young Seaman O'Riley gave him the good luck kiss and told the crew, "The reactor will come back on shortly, no sweat. It just needs a good talking to and Sean O'Riley has the luck of the Irish."

After a bit of nervous laughter from the crew she told Seaman O'Riley to open the door. The instant his hand touched the door, the reactor came back on line. She grabbed O'Riley and swung him around three times in a dancing motion. The crew was silent.

The Exec asked, "Captain, how'd you know?"

"When you've been Captain for as long as I have . . . ," was her answer. This time she laughed out loud. Then added, "Let's go find that submarine, Mister. Check everything and let me know if we're still ready to get underway."

When she got to her quarters, just as she had suspected, no Mr. Michael. She sent for Seaman O'Riley and when he arrived she asked, "Have you seen your hero Mr. Michael?"

"I don't know anyone by that name, Captain, and ma'am, you're my hero," he answered, and then said, "Captain, I must not be as brave as you think because I was really scared until you kissed me. Thank you so much for the courage."

"Scared is what makes the hero. If you have no fear to overcome, you're not a hero, you're just some plain old dumb guy who does a great deed. And son, you ain't dumb. You're my hero." She put her hand on his shoulder and nudged him out the door. "Now get outta here, boy, and go back to work," she said in the same tone she would use to tell her son to go wash the car.

"Captain, we're ready to get underway. Captain . . . wake up," it was the Exec.

"We're ready to get underway. The weather between here and Pearl is perfect, not that we'll get to enjoy any of it, but it's nice to know what's going on in the real world. And there's a Mister Michael topside wanting to see you."

"I'll be right up there. Scrub half of the scheduled drills. The crew will need the rest. This one's gonna be a helluva voyage," she said and thought to herself, "The same dream twice. Okay, but not three times. I'll put an end to Mister Michael right now."

Once topside, she saw Mister Michael standing near the brow. He gave her a sharp salute. She returned the salute and said, "Mister, we don't need you on this cruise. I don't care who sent you. Go back and tell him that we can do very well on our own."

"But Captain, that's exactly what I came to tell you. Your prayers have been answered. You know what to do. I'm here to tell you that I'm not just a dream.

It has been a pleasure serving with you," he said. "If only in your dreams."

He was half way up the plank on his way to the pier when she asked, "Why did I have to dream the same thing twice?"

"Hey, once for you and once for Mrs. Brown," he replied. "And my boss wishes you a Bon Voyage."

"Who is your boss?" she asked, stressing the "is".

"You know who my boss is." He stressed the "know" as he saluted her.

She returned the salute and something unusual happened. When Mister Michael was finishing his salute he put his hands to his lips and blew her a kiss and said, "Remember me." Then he was gone, as fast as the Roadrunner, without the Beep-Beep and the dust.

"Captain, that's the strangest person I've ever seen," said Seaman O'Riley, who was standing the topside watch.

"Yes he's strange, but stranger things are yet to come. Bon Voyage indeed! He's going to scare my crew half to death. I think I'll go ashore with the crew in Pearl, I haven't seen a good fistfight in years," she was muttering this last part while walking away.

Seaman O'Riley could swear he heard music as he watched her walk, or skate or glide or whatever it is that she does.

She turned around and smiled at the seaman with a smile that would light up the entire Island of Alcatraz. She wondered what her son was doing at this moment, and then thought, "This kid doesn't know strange. By the time this voyage is over, there will be two of us who will believe we've been kissed by an angel."

ONE WHALE OF A TORPEDO

Weird things are seen on a submarine,
But the weirdest that I can cite
Was in September, as I remember,
When the sub and the whale had a fight.

The sky was blue, as the sun shone through
But the waters looked creamy white.
We were down below, sixty feet or so,
When the sub and the whale had a fight.

The seas were smooth as an old bear's tooth,
And as quiet as the spider's bite.
Then came the thump, a grating bump,
And the sub and the whale had a fight.

Then came the word "surface", we heard,
One order we didn't take light.
Once on top, came the word "all stop"
After the sub and the whale had a fight

After looking around, we took her down,
And the skipper said so contrite.
"No damage here, nothing to fear,
Just the sub and the whale had a fight."

That was not the end of our dear friend,
And by swimming with all his might,
He stayed by our side, far and wide
After he and the sub had a fight.

Everyday, he was in our way,
Now to the left, now to the right,
He would ram into us, and kick up a fuss.
Again the sub and the whale had a fight.

And for all we did, we could not be rid

Of this fish causing our plight.
The damage was worse than thought at first,
After the sub and the whale had a fight.

So we fired torpedoes straight for the nose
In hopes this would make him take flight.
But to our surprise, this lit up his eyes.
We had thoughts of another fight.

He screamed aloud, gave cigars to the crowd
And splashed up and down with delight.
He thinks, I thought, maybe, the torpedo is his baby,
So did the sub and the whale have a fight?

MISS LORIE, THE BADGE AND THE BUTTERFLY

The old man walked into the jewelry store. He was a little stooped over. Short slivers of silver hair stuck out from under his baseball cap. His overalls were worn, but impeccably neat. Behind him was his twelve year-old grandson, Patrick. They stopped at the counter and asked for the owner, Miss Lorie.

Miss Lorie came to the counter. "What can I do for you, sir?" She was a beautiful young lady wearing a pink pants suit and high heels. She could be dressed for an evening at the theater, except she was wearing high fashion sunglasses. It made her look more like she was a little girl playing dress-up.

"I would like to buy my wife something special for Christmas and she said I must get it from you. We were in here two years ago and you sold us a pendant that had some diamonds on it that you called 'Hi Ho, off to work I go'," the old man said.

"I remember that pendant," Miss Lorie said, smiling. "I hope she liked it."

"She loved it, everyone loved it. Her Godchild loved it so much that my wife gave it to her for her sixteenth birthday. She says I have no taste, and insisted that I ask you to select the gift. The gift was supposed to be for her seventy-fifth birthday, but the hurricane forced some friends of ours to evacuate and they needed some money to get back from Tennessee so we loaned them the money.

"They couldn't pay us back afore the birthday, but made it in time for Christmas," he explained. "That's why it's so special, it's for both occasions. I saved a long time for this."

"And me! I put in my grass cutting money, too, Grandpa," said Patrick.

"You, too," said Grandpa. He opened a leather pouch and took out some bills. "This was my marble bag when I was a kid." He handed Miss Lorie the money.

"I remember your wife now. You had that same bag the last time you were here," Miss Lorie replied. "How's your wife? She should have come with you."

"Grandma is very, sick," said Patrick. "They sent her home from the hospital but she still has to stay in bed for a while. She says she'll come next time."

The old man, standing behind Patrick, made a gesture for Miss Lorie not to ask any more questions. "Patrick, go get my glasses outta the truck."

After Patrick left, the old man explained to Miss Lorie that the boy didn't know the extent of his grandma's illness and this was probably her last Christmas.

Miss Lorie expressed sympathy and then counted the money. "One hundred and fifty one dollars. Wait here for a minute. Let me see what we have. I'll bring something to show you."

Miss Lorie got up and went behind the counter. She returned with a sparkler.

"Look at this necklace. We got this in a special deal and it's something your wife will love," Miss Lorie had on her best smile.

"Well, it's beautiful, but we don't have enough money for that. It has five big diamonds. Those are real diamonds?" asked the old man, with raised eyebrows.

"Yes, they're real. We got'em in a special package deal because we bought a large quantity for the holidays," Miss Lorie said, "and this week we've advertised that we pay the sales tax. You're lucky your friends didn't pay you back until now."

"Wrap it up. I'm sure you're getting the worst of this deal," he said.

In the truck, driving home, Patrick said, "That necklace had a price tag of four hundred dollars. I saw it when we came in."

"I know," the old man said. "Even if I told you a thousand times that we don't take charity, I couldn't hurt that lady's feelings or deny her the pleasure she'd get from doing something good for somebody. Apparently that feeling is worth more to her than the necklace. And you know what's even better'n that? It didn't cost us nothing but pride to give her such pleasure. Ain't we got too much pride anyhow?"

Three months later a letter came for Miss Lorie. It had no return address. She opened the envelope and found a picture of an elderly lady wearing the necklace. The lady was in a wheelchair and looked like she just came from the beauty salon.

The letter said, "Miss Lorie, my grandmother passed away last week and Grandpa says to write to you and send this picture so you could always have that great feeling when you see the happiness you gave to grandma. She wore the necklace and bragged about your good taste and told everyone to go to your store and ask for you.

"Grandpa hammered a nail in the wall of my room and hung the necklace there. He said that it would remind me of the true meaning of giving. We thank you very much and Grandpa says that when you get to heaven Grandma will find you and thank you too. Love Grandpa and Patrick." A bunch of Xs and Os were at the end.

Two years later, a package came to the store marked "Attn: Miss Lorie." She went into her office, opened the package and found the necklace with a letter from Patrick.

"Thank you for the loan of the necklace. Grandpa died last week, but he had told me to send you the necklace because you would find someone else that needed it as much as we did and that it had served its purpose here. He also asked that you tell nobody the name of the benefactor or it wouldn't count. He told me not to send the necklace back until I understood this. I am fifteen years old now and I know what he meant. Thank you for your kindness. Love Grandma, Grandpa and Patrick."

Miss Lorie put on her "Hollywood" sunglasses and left her office.

Mr. Landry got out of the elevator on the twentieth floor and went in through the door marked Administrative Negotiator. "Tell your boss Mr. Landry is here," he told the secretary.

The secretary recognized Mr. Landry as the company's newest and most important client. Something big was in the offing. She went into the private office and nodded her head towards the door, "Excuse me, 'Mr. Big' is here, Patrick," she said.

"He's a little early," Patrick said, and as he looked at his appointment calendar he noticed the next day would be the tenth anniversary of his grandpa's death. "I'll be right out, please send in a coffee tray. Are we about through here, sir?" Patrick asked his boss, Mr. David Robichaux.

"When I'm in this chair, I'm just keeping it warm for him," Mr. Robichaux said. "I thought you were a little too honest when you first came to us because you lost as many deals as you completed, but you have attracted the attention of the biggest entrepreneur in the state. This is a make or break deal. If you sign this deal, I'll be a believer. If not, well, we'll see. I know you like it here, so, good luck, my boy."

Mr. Landry walked into the office and noticed a glass wall behind the desk. "What a great view of the Mississippi River, Patrick." he said.

"Yes, here we are twenty stories up on a man made mountain looking down on a river that just laughs at our attempts to control it. Every year it jumps the levee somewhere and lets us know that we may be high but not so mighty. It is both an exhilarating and humbling view. Sir, if you'll look just off to the left you can see the French Quarter. I love it up here," the young exec said. "Please take a seat. I'm having the proposals brought up here now. Would you like a cup of coffee?"

"Yes, that would be great. I must apologize for being a bit early; there was not as much traffic as I had anticipated."

As Mr. Landry looked around the spacious office he saw a wall covered with degrees and certificates. He got up and walked to the wall and said, "I see here that you are a very learned fellow and quite respected as well. If you live up to your reputation for fair and honest treatment of your clients we may have the biggest deal in this company's history. I'm sure there are others in this company as honest as you, but you come so highly recommended. You must be proud of your reputation."

"That thar's muh braggin wall you're alooking at right now," Patrick said in a mock cowboy drawl. Then in a normal voice, "Every now and then when a deal falls through and I feel that I didn't do enough, I come to this wall and pick myself up.

"I am very proud of my reputation, sir, but I owe it all to my grandfather, he deserves all the credit for what I have become. My father was a soldier and died in the Middle East War so my grandfather raised me and gave me all of his morals and work ethics. Here is a picture of him on this wall." The young man said, pointing to the opposite wall where a dozen or so pictures were hanging.

"Are all these pictures of your family?" Mr. Landry asked, walking to the wall. "The picture of the old man is my grandfather and the lady in the wheel chair wearing a necklace is my grandmother. The picture in between them, the lady with the Hollywood sunglasses, is Miss Lorie; she's not related to me, but really belongs there. Below that is a picture of my wife and baby and my father and mother and my two cousins and their families."

"Who is this Miss Lorie?" Mr. Landry asked, really interested in the beautiful lady in the picture. "She looks like a movie star with those big sunglasses."

"I really don't know her, she owns a jewelry store, I only met her once when I was a kid, but she was a very nice lady.

"Every Christmas she goes to an old folk's home and offers free hairdos for some of the ladies. Then she has them wear some of her jewelry and put on a fashion show for the residents. They take pictures that are placed in fashion magazines.

The nurses that push the wheel chairs around are young ladies from the local colleges and they are decked out too. Everyone has a good time and although it is too late to get the pictures in the Christmas editions, they come out in the Valentines and Mother's day issues," Patrick said.

"That sounds like a great campaign, but how does that rate a picture on your wall?" asked Mr. Landry.

"Well, in an interview for one of her fashion shows she said she got the inspiration from a picture of an elderly lady in a wheel chair wearing one of her necklaces. That lady was my grandma, see her there with the necklace.

"Miss Lorie had sold that necklace to my Grandpa for a ridiculously low price," explained Patrick. "Grandpa said that it was the best example of the spirit of Christmas he ever saw. I clipped Miss Lorie's picture out of the magazine and put it next to Grandma. They would be proud to have it there."

"That was a very interesting story. I would like another cup of coffee before you tell me about this wall," Mr. Landry said, pointing to the wall facing the desk. It was a blank wall with a nail sticking out of it; a butterfly was mounted on the nail.

"What is that all about? Some kind of trophy perhaps?"

"Not exactly," Patrick replied, "Grandpa put that nail on the wall of my bedroom when Grandma died and hung the necklace there. I was just a kid at the time and Grandpa said it would remind me that giving and receiving are sometimes equal partners. He said that sometimes you are giving by receiving.

"A while after Grandpa died I sent the necklace back to Miss Lorie. It was his request that I do this after I fully understood the meaning. I put the butterfly on the nail because it is also a reminder of another very special lesson from Grandpa's favorite story. When I went to college I took the nail with me. When I got this job I hammered it in that wall.

"He once told me if you put all the butterflies that ever lived on a straight line, together, from the North Pole to the South Pole, facing east, and have them all leap into the air at once, the Earth would stop turning for an instant. He said every time I see a single butterfly I would remember that the least thing I do causes unseen events.

"That nail holds my life together. It guarantees that you will get a fair deal from me every time. It guarantees a peaceful untroubled life with plenty of happiness for people around me. That nail is the reason you are here talking to me.

"Sometimes when I complete a big deal and get to feeling full of myself and start thinking that I deserve all I have, I will look out of the window at the river and then look over to the wall at that nail. That brings me back to the realization that I am not such a big shot. I didn't get here by myself.

"That's all I can say about it, except that it's not just a nail." Patrick said and then apologized for being so long winded.

"Quite alright, I understand you a lot better now. My curiosity is more than mere etiquette. I didn't get where I am today by talking about myself, I have learned to ask questions and listen for answers. Over the years I've become an astute judge of the sincerity of a person . . . to the nth degree. You have convinced me that your reputation is not just for show," Mr. Landry said, just as they were bringing in the proposals.

"Perfect timing, I believe we are going to do a lot of business together."

He walked to the wall and looked at the movie star in the picture once more. "Why would she sell the necklace so cheaply? What started all this? What's with those sunglasses?" he wondered. He had a million questions. He would have to ask Patrick for the name of the jewelry store so he could see this lady for himself.

For meeting her only once, she must be some kind of an angel or at least a saint, to have had such an impact on this young man's life. He wondered if Patrick saw the necklace as Miss Lorie's butterfly or if he was aware of how that butterfly story fit that scenario perfectly. She is a beautiful lady and a mysterious one, too. She had almost made him forget about the proposals. . . . Allllmost

The fashion magazine reporter, Louise, was sitting across the desk from Miss Lorie. It wasn't a large office. The walls were covered with pictures of well-groomed older women in wheelchairs with beautiful young ladies in attendance.

"Well, Lorie, you called me and said you would finally tell me about the Grandma Fashion Show. What made you change your mind? I've been after the story for almost ten years," Louise said.

"I just figured out a way to tell the story without dishonoring a request from a young admirer. I want to affect others the same way I was affected," said Miss Lorie.

"A Mr. Landry came in the store a few days ago, you know him as Mr. Big, and he told me about a young friend of mine that I'd been wondering about for sometime.

Mr. Landry told me that I would be extremely proud of the young man."

"I didn't know that you knew Mr. Big," Louise said, interrupting Miss Lorie.

"Well, I do and we did lunch a few times, but no more about that right now, let's get to the story you came here for," said Miss Lorie.

"Mr. Landry told me about my young friend, Patrick, and a nail his grandpa put in the wall to hold his grandma's necklace after she died. The nail now holds a butterfly to remind him of another one of his grandpa's stories about the least action causing an unknown effect somewhere. All interesting stories about the young man and his honesty and how something I did had an impact on his life." Miss Lorie was telling the story almost bragging, as she would if Patrick were her son.

"I was sitting right here where I am now, reading a magazine. I think it was the Readers Digest, but I'm not sure. Anyway the name of the magazine doesn't really matter, it was the story that I was reading that started this whole thing. I remember it was on my twentieth birthday and my brother Bobby had just made me a partner.

"It was about a little boy, Rickey, who asked his mother for a few dollars to buy a Christmas present for a friend. Money was hard to come by, but the boy said that he would accept the money in place of a Christmas gift. He was an exceptional kid so the mother gave in because Christmas comes only once a year.

"Rickey walked the two blocks into town and stopped at the department store. He asked the lady to see a coat. He said it was a Christmas present for his best friend.

"The clerk, who knew Rickey, asked which friend and was told that it was for Little David, his desk-mate in the second grade in school. He explained that all Little David had was a beat up old sweater and he was cold when they walked to school.

"The boy put five dollars on the counter and asked the lady if she had a good coat for that price. The saleslady came back with a coat and wrapped it up and told the young man that he had enough change to buy candy for himself and Little David.

"When the boy got home and his mother unwrapped the package, she saw the price tag. The coat cost twelve dollars. She went back to the store and asked the lady if there had been a mistake. There was no error. The lady explained that everyone in town knew Rickey and Little David. This was just payback for two great kids and payback felt so good, the feeling was worth more than the money. Everyone in the store had chipped in.

"I'd just finished reading that story when an old man and his grandson came in the store and asked to see me. I had tears in my eyes from reading that story so I had to put on my sunglasses to hide it. The old man said he wanted to buy a gift for his wife and he handed me one hundred and fifty one dollars. The necklace I sold him was worth about four hundred dollars, but I wanted to see if that feeling was real. It was, and it was a pretty good feeling, but I didn't think it was worth two hundred and fifty dollars. At least not until three months later when I received a letter from the grandson and a picture of his grandma wearing the necklace. I got goose bumps all over when I saw the picture and I still do every time I see it. There it is hanging on the wall. Patrick's Grandma had passed and the necklace was hung on the wall.

"I knew I couldn't do that every Christmas because I have partners, so I thought of the old folks in the nursing homes. I pay the college girls for modeling with the older ladies, the older ladies get a beauty shop treatment, get to wear fine jewelry and get their pictures in fashion magazines with the young ladies and we actually make money from our advertisements. Not much money, but it keeps my partners happy.

"They say it keeps me out of their hair for a couple of months a year," Miss Lorie said, finishing up her story and getting out of her chair to indicate that the interview was over.

"That's quite a story and I'm sure it will inspire others to be more charitable.

Let's get some pictures for the magazine," Louise said.

"That's the only reason I told the story and please don't make it any bigger than I told it. Wait, let me put my sunglasses on," Miss Lorie said.

Bobby walked into the office just as the reporter was leaving. "Did you tell the whole story, Sis? Remember it won't count if you tell the name of the benefactor."

"Nope, I left out the part where the nursing home gives us the name of a terminal patient who gets to keep the special necklace at the end of the fashion show.

"Isn't it amazing, we've given that necklace away eight times and we keep getting it back? None of the families have ever kept it. Even though it was theirs to do whatever they want, they keep giving it back in time for the next show. People really do understand the meaning of Christmas.

"I don't know if I can stand anymore of these goose bumps," Miss Lorie said. Wiping her eyes, she looked up at Bobby and smiled.

"I'll bet. Just talking about it and your eyes are red right now," Bobby said.

"Well, I guess, I'll just have to get used to wearing these inside the store." Miss Lorie was mumbling to herself as she touched her sunglasses. Whatever happened to Little David and his pal Rickey, she wondered.

She got up and walked into the store still wearing the sunglasses and a big smile looking like a movie star. Thanks to Mr. Big she now had a concept of the butterfly on Patrick's nail, so she kind of felt like a movie star, too.

A few weeks later, Miss Lorie got a letter from Mr. Big. In it he explained that he had a detective agency track down the boys in the story she had read and that it was a little difficult to find them because it was an old story. They found a Monsignor Lee and a Rabbi Weiss who, with pride, updated the story from beginning to end.

They said that an old man lived across the street from Little David. His son had been a fireman and had died in the line of duty. His son was somewhat of a local hero even though his heroism was achieved in another town. If the old man had had any grandchildren they would be Little David's age, so he regarded Little David as kin. The old man didn't have much money and what he did have usually went to paying the rent and groceries and an occasional doctor's bill. He was just a regular lonely old guy.

Little David wanted to be a fireman like the old man's son. He had pictures of fire trucks on the wall in his bedroom.

He even had badge number 792 that the old man had given him for his sixth birthday. It had belonged to the old man's son. Little David never took the badge off; he wore it to school, he even wore it on his pajamas at night. He was going to be a fireman. It didn't weaken his desire any when the old man told him heroic tales about firemen carrying babies out of burning buildings, bringing people back to life with CPR, rescuing cats from tall trees and especially riding on the fire truck with the sirens going full blast.

There was a small cedar tree in Little David's front yard and he and his friend Rickey decided to decorate it for Christmas. The old man gave them a string of Christmas tree lights and went around town with them collecting old cans to hang on the tree. They had some evaporated milk cans, a few beer cans and some cream style corn cans, all different colors and sizes. Somebody had given them a couple of ping-pong balls. Everything went on the tree. It had a Star of David on top, courtesy of Rabbi Weiss, the neighborhood good guy. Everybody loved the two kids.

The townspeople came by and remarked how beautiful the tree was. And when some came a second time they brought an ornament for the tree, so that after a while it became the best-decorated tree in town. The two kids stood for a long time at night looking at the tree. Rickey said that he could see the angels floating around inspecting the tree. Little David could see them too, but his were riding around the tree on fire trucks.

They felt lucky to have such great friends and neighbors. They were poor and didn't know it. They were rich and everyone knew it.

It was finally Christmas day and Little David answered the knock at the door and saw Rickey with a present under his arm. He handed the package over to Little David.

He immediately tore it open to find a beautiful coat. He tried it on and it fit perfectly. Perfectly meaning that it was a little too big so that he could grow into it for a couple of years. Then use it for a third year when it would be a little too small.

Little David went into his room and came back with a little package wrapped in torn grocery bag paper and tied with kite string. He handed it to Rickey and said, "Merry Christmas. I hope you like it. It's the best thing I can give to my best friend."

Rickey opened the little package and saw the badge numbered 792.

Little David's mama ran across the street to tell the old man about the present Little David gave to Rickey. This would be the old man's best Christmas ever. He knew how much the boy loved that badge and what it would take to give it up.

The two boys were sitting in church later that day and when the priest stood up to give his sermon he said, "This is going to go down on record as the shortest sermon in Catholic history. We're blessed today to have with us Dave and Rick Amen."

Everyone stood and clapped, even Rabbi Weiss, who was attending the Catholic mass that day, compliments of a personal invitation from Monsignor Lee.

Hymns were sung a little louder that day and the collection plate was filled.

Years later on a spring day in the little town in Iowa, the sun was shining and the breeze was blowing. God had to be looking down on the little town, smiling.

The newly ordained priest was standing outside of the new fire station talking to the town's youngest fire chief. "Thanks for having me come down to bless your firehouse, Dave," said Father Rick. "I see 'Ole 792' on your hat. It looks worn out." "It oughtta be, I've worn it every day since you gave it back to me as a birthday present," the fire chief said. "Was that eighteen years ago, already?"

"Probably. Anyway, I had to give it back to you; you borrowed it from me every day. And besides you looked naked without it," Father Rick said, "How did you talk the mayor into letting you wear it on your uniform? It has the name of a different town in a different state."

"Everybody in town said they would vote him out of office if he didn't let me wear Ole 792," Dave replied.

Jamie, Father Rick's younger brother, was chasing a beautiful Monarch butterfly that was fluttering around the priest and the fire chief at the ceremony.

Then the letter went on to say that Mr. Big had to add his version of a fitting ending. He wrote the closure for Miss Lorie. He was really into this thing.

He wrote that Rickey and Little David walked into the fire station with their arms on each other's shoulder without Hollywood sunglasses on because neither knew of the necklace, the picture, the nail, the hairdo at the old folks home or the fashion mags that came about because of the Christmas coat and the badge numbered 792.

There was also an investigator's personal side note attached to the letter:

"Jamie was the only one aware of the butterfly fluttering around and landing on the fire chief's badge. He, also not knowing all the events, nor ever having heard Patrick's butterfly story, never gave it a thought.

After all, it was only one little butterfly and any connection would be way too subtle, but wouldn't that be a perfect ending to the story if he had?"

Mr. Landry ended the letter by asking Miss Lorie if she would marry him at Superbowl XLIV in Miami. He had already reserved the spot. It was signed "Mr. Big," her pet name for him. She said that fits the biggest businessman in the state.

Miss Lorie grabbed a handful of air and pulled it down to punctuate her words as she said out loud, "YES! And we will name our first son after the quarterback Drew Brees."

WOLF GOES TO REHAB
III & IV FOR A. M. CATOIR

John Scott was sitting in the French Quarter district police station interrogation room answering the big question.

"You ask me if I did it. What can I say? Yes, yes I did it. But, before you judge me, before you condemn me, let me tell you the whole story. You must know that I'm not the monster that everyone thinks I am. Yes, I killed. But I killed for reasons you wouldn't understand. Still, I'll try to explain. This isn't an excuse mind you, I just want it on record, you know, to explain why I did what I did. You see I had no choice. I had to." He was trying to explain the unexplainable to himself as much as to the detectives.

Scott was being charged with the multiple counts of murder and mutilation that had happened over the past few months. The newspapers were calling for the resignation of the police chief. They wanted a full FBI probe into the incompetence of the police department. They suspected a cover-up.

"It started with the dreams," he said. "That was the beginning, the beginning of a nightmare from which there was no escape. It was always the same. I could see the full moon behind the clouds. It was like something out of one of those old horror movies, you know, really weird but so real. It was like I wasn't doing it, I was watching it being done.

"I remember the first time. The poor old man never had a chance. I saw the blood everywhere. Then I tasted it. It tasted so good. I just could not help myself. Suddenly, there I was, slashing and tearing and drinking his blood. Soon I was consumed with a lust that I had never known before. A bloodlust.

"I awoke the next morning with the memory of the dream vivid in my mind. I didn't mention the dream to my wife as I was convinced that it was just a dream. I went to work that day troubled, yet convinced just the same that it was merely a dream. After that my life became everything the newspapers wrote about. Dream after dream continued. As did murder after murder. My dreams were real life.

"Still I remained convinced that it was some sort of psychic episode, that there was no way I could be responsible for the terrible things happening in town. Convinced, that is, until I could no longer ignore what I knew to be true. And even though the people in town would not say the word, I knew there was only one creature capable of the horror being brought upon the town. Werewolf.

"It was in April that I first began to notice the signs and see the evidence. I awoke after one particularly bad dream. In the dream I was stalking a policeman. I killed and ate him. When I awoke the next morning, my bedroom window was open and there was a shred of blue cloth lying on the floor. It had blood on it. It was part of a uniform. There was also mud tracked on the floor coming from the open window.

"That was when she had started telling me how troubled my sleep had been. I knew it was true but I didn't know how much it affected her. Also I noticed that everything that was ever of interest to me seemed trivial. There was also a tension between us akin to an unspoken rage. My brain was one constant hot flash.

"She told me that I was acting strangely and I found myself increasingly agitated with her. What could I say to her? 'To hell with you.' I loved her and I didn't like the thought of hurting her. She was the only thing in my life that I could count on. The only constant I could rely on. She was my life. I loved her more than I could ever say. But you ask me why, then, did I kill her? Because I had to kill her.

"You see, I woke up one night in the middle of a dream, in my bed alone, she wasn't there. It was the opening of a window that had aroused me. That's when I saw her covered in blood and looking like a diseased animal. A rabid dog.

"For a moment I just stood there stunned, but then everything started making a crazy sort of sense. She was the werewolf, not me. She was living my dreams or maybe I was dreaming her life. Maybe she whispered in my ear at night while I was asleep. I don't know. I told you it was mixed up but it made sense to me.

"When I confronted her, she admitted it all, and that started a fight. The fight didn't last long, a lot of scratching and biting, which ended when I stabbed her with a piece of silverware that was on the table.

"Then you guys came in and you know the rest of the story," he said.

They put John in the hospital for the criminally insane until his trial and he would probably have stayed there for the rest of his life. The police thought he had made up that story to avoid the death sentence so there was not much interest in proving or disproving his account. He had a good story and he stuck to it. At any rate he would be out of circulation, case closed, money saved. Great police PR.

However, television reporters have considerably more cash and time to devote to a story. They also have that device known as a nose for news, a special talent on loan from God, and once on the scent it is like a shark in a blood bath.

There was DNA testing of the victims and blood testing of John's wife with the results confirming John's story. He stayed in the asylum for over two years and was finally released and ordered to rehab. It was great television PR.

John was sitting on a bench in Washington Artillery Park in the French Quarter of New Orleans waiting for the advent of the full moon. He figured he had about another fifteen minutes before the moon came out. He looked like a gypsy in the old movies with his mustache and beard not well trimmed, but just neat enough so that nobody would mistake him for a hobo. He had on a gray suit and a white shirt, missing a tie. It was hanging out of his coat pocket.

His black shoes were highly polished. He was dressed like a businessman after a long hard day at the office. He'd been acting strange of late, nothing really bad, but he knew he had reason to be concerned. Would it happen to him, also? Two months had past since the ordeal with his wife. Or was that six months ago, or maybe a year. He couldn't exactly remember. That was another thing; his memory was going in and out. Mostly in, but frequently out.

A young lady hurriedly passed by the bench on her way home from work trying to get out of the park before the sun went down. Lots of strange things were happening these days. Can hardly trust anyone.

John Scott noticed her beautiful legs, but that was all because he now felt an inner calling, an urge to howl at the moon, which had not yet come into view. As far as women were concerned, he had always been considered a sort of wolf, but the feelings he had now were different. He couldn't exactly put his finger on it, but they were definitely different.

Last full moon, his neighbor had the police come to quiet him down. He'd been baying at the moon. He took three sleeping pills, put duct tape over his mouth and went to sleep. That had to be related to his wife's wolf bite. Or something.

He was in therapy for some related problems, like eating Alpo for breakfast every morning. Rehab was helping. Thanks to Lisa, one of the therapists, he could now more or less control his eating habits. As for howling at the moon, he was determined to beat that instinct this very night with some of the tips given him by Brian, the towel boy at rehab. Rehab was good; he no longer chased cats up trees thanks to Frankie. And Katlin cured him of chasing cars when she ran over his foot in the rehab parking lot. Katherine, the boss, had been reading a book written by the "dog whisperer" during the lull between patients. She was full of good tips. Everyone at the Covington "Care" rehab center was helping.

Mickey O'Hare, the policeman on night patrol, came up to the bench and told John he didn't want any trouble that night. John assured the officer that he was in the park so that if he couldn't control his howling, at least nobody would be disturbed.

He added that he was pretty sure he could control it.

John felt an urge deep inside his body. It was not like the howling urge, although that was still there. This was more of a grabbing, gripping urge—it was powerful almost completely overshadowing the urge to bay at the moon. It was tearing at him and the moon was not yet in view. What would happen when the moon came out? He was scaring himself with these thoughts. He was really scared that one night he would be shot and in the morning he would wake up dead. Wake up dead! See, he was losing his mind. What was going on here? He was really confused.

Just then another young lady passed by on her way home. John followed her with his eyes until she got to the gateway of the park. He was trying to ignore what was happening to him, but all of a sudden he saw the tip of the moon coming over the top of the trees and he jumped up and headed for the gateway. The thing he feared most was happening to him. He couldn't fight this thing, He thought of all the tricks they taught him in rehab, he thought of his mother, his sister and anybody else that he cared for deeply. Nothing was working. This urge was tearing at his insides. He tried howling at the moon, but that was useless, he was overcome. He gave in.

The next day the jailer open the cell door and said, "OK, Scotty, time to see the judge." He led the way to the courtroom.

"Hear ye, hear ye, hear ye, city court is now in session, Judge Jerry Thomas presiding. All rise." That was the clerk, Jamie O'Hare, the policeman's brother.

The Judge came in and said, "Please will everyone be seated."

"What's the first case on the docket, Harry?" That was Jamie's nickname.

"The city versus John Scott case number 55114," Jamie said. And then added, "Prisoner, come to the bar."

"You are charged with article 219. How do you plead?" asked the judge "Guilty your honor, but I vaguely remember the incident. The urge was more than I could handle. I just went crazy. I am so sorry and I apologize to everyone." John sounded sincere.

"Since you are still in rehab, you'll only have to pay a hundred dollars fine and spend the next six full moon nights in jail," the judge said. "Pay the cashier on your way out and check with the jailer to see when you must report to him. I' m only being so lenient because your rehab counselor assures me that she has some new techniques from the dog whisperer that addresses your affliction. You should be so ashamed of yourself, Scotty, urinating on a fire hydrant in public," then added with a big smile, "Bad dog. Bad, dog."

A FINAL SOLUTION AT LAST
FOR JEFF 990

Albert Frankein Stein Ogre the IV, aka "Big Al", was sitting at his computer working on a Global warming theory. He was the world's foremost authority on the subject.

He was retracing the steps that were taken to reduce global warming. Everything had seemed to fail.

There was the replacement of all light bulbs with a cooler source of light, but it took more energy to dispose of the newer lights because of the chemicals involved. The oceans rose an inch.

Next came solar panels on top of every house, but then since electricity was free, every home in the world had an air conditioner in every room exhausting hot air and was never turned off global warming continued. The oceans rose an inch.

Then he called a world meeting and had every country agree to "Cap and Trade", but that only shifted carbon emissions from one area to another. The oceans rose an inch.

Next all of the cows in the world were slaughtered because of flatulence, but that meant people were now eating vegetables, mostly rice and beans, which increased human flatulence and global warming continued. The oceans rose an inch.

After that, all gasoline cars were banned and only electric cars were produced, but since electricity was free everyone in the world had their own personal car and the miles they drove increased and the energy it took to keep up the infrastructure offset any energy savings. The oceans rose an inch.

Next he had all of the Eskimos quit making igloos from the ice cap, but when they used wood it depleted the rain forest. The oceans rose an inch.

Then disaster struck. There was a black substance in the air that was conducting the heat from the sun. None of the greatest scientific minds could figure out what the substance was. None, that is, except Big Al. He came to the conclusion that it was being caused by the residue of the deleted words on a computer. It had never been noticed before because there were relatively few computers in the world, but since the cost of computers was low everyone in the world owned one. That increased the words deleted a trillion times a trillion times. Those deleted words had to go somewhere. Logic could not escape him. He was not known as the world's greatest mind because of a lack of imagination. It separated him from the flock.

He called another world summit and explained his theory. The whole world applauded. He was awarded the Nobel Prize.

The media groveled at his feet; thrills went up their legs at the mere mention of his name. He was the "Man".

Now every computer had to have a recycle bin flash drive, a tiny removable device that would capture all deletions from a computer. Recycling trucks would pass by every home on a weekly basis and pick up the flash drives and bring them to a disposal area where they would be buried.

Soon there was no more room for the flash drives in the dump, but Big Al had the solution. Dump them in the Grand Canyon. That was a great idea that lasted for about a month until the Canyon was completely filled.

The Chinese had a similar problem that they solved by dumping along each side of the Great Wall. After two months of dumping the whole length of the Great Wall was a mile wide.

Big Al had the solution ready for the world. Dump the flash drives in the Mariannas Trench. That could never be filled. The world again marveled at his logic.

At the next official reading of the ocean it had risen two feet. The earth was in the last stages of complete destruction. Something had to be done immediately. Global warming, although imperceptible on a thermometer, was threatening mankind.

The melting of the ice cap had to be stopped. The rising of the ocean problem had to be solved. He would find the solution, all of mankind depended on him.

He heard a commotion in the living room and went out to find his son, Al the V, aka Li'l Al, refilling his aquarium after having cleaned it out.

"Don't fill it all the way to the top or when you put the marbles in it will rise above the top and spill out on the carpet like it did last time," he told his son.

"Don't worry, Pop, I learned my lesson from the last time," he replied. "And Mom said I could move it away from under the air conditioning vent because one of my fish froze to death," he added.

Big Al went back to his computer and thought for a while and then it came to him. The whole solution came from his conversation with Li'l Al. His son had given him the solution and never realized it. Why hadn't he thought of that before now? Probably because it was so simple and he was trained to think on a higher scale. From the mouth of babes comes wisdom. This would get him another Nobel Prize. He would share it with Li'l Al.

He grabbed his hat and was heading for the door when his wife, Skipper, stopped him and asked where he was going.

"I have to get to Washington, I have found the solution to the whole global warming problem," he said, "call Madam X Speaker, she turned green after the 2010 elections and I'll need her support. Tell her I'm coming."

"That's nice dear. Don't forget to take your gas mask, that black stuff is getting thicker," she said

He put on his gas mask and ran to his electric limo. "She's right, it does seem to be thicker than usual. I'll have to ask them to increase the flash drive recycling pick-ups," he thought, "right after I tell them that we are going to circle the Ice Caps with air conditioners. At last, a final solution."

HOW MY SACRIFICE SAVES NEW ORLEANS

As told to
Benton Phillips
For the Savage Nation

The story you are about to read is true. Just because you won't believe it doesn't make it any less true. The names have been omitted for reasons that will be explained at the end of the story. Certain passages have been flourished a little to stress a point, but not so much as to change the facts.

I guess it all started back in 1975 when my wife asked if her brother could come stay with us until he got on his feet. I couldn't come up with a reason good enough not to say yes (At least not good enough to keep peace in the family.) so I agreed. What she failed to tell me was that he was a victim of polio and would probably never get back on his feet.

In all fairness to the man I must say he helped my daughter with her homework and drove her to school and even taught her how to be a good republican. (If there is such an animal.) But on the other hand . . . I could help her with her homework, my wife could drive her to school and the school could make her a good democrat.

Well, my friends, if you ever lived with a relative I am sure you know that there is a lack of privacy, disruptions in scheduling, disputes over the television and just plain botherations above the ankles and below the neck. So in 1995 I started praying for him to find a place of his own. I guess that GOD got tired of my praying for the same thing every night for two years, so he answered my prayer. Literally.

GOD said, "My boy, I have sent your brother-in-law to you so you could learn humility and patience, but you are a slow learner so he will be with you until you die. He is under my personal protection and I will bring the wrath of heaven down on your head if you attempt to thwart my plans."

Now, before you start saying that I am crazy, let me tell you that anything you can say about this, I have already said. I ignored this voice and considered it just a figment of an over active imagination caused by an intense desire for internal peace and harmony.

So I continued my nightly prayers and just as a little lagniappe I would drop subtle hints. After a couple of more years the hints became suggestions, but still to no avail, the situation remained unresolved. I then resorted to gentle prodding for a few years and that didn't work either.

In late summer of 2005 we bought a house outside of the city. My brother-in-law decided that it would be too long of a drive into the city so he got himself an apartment.

I was elated. And that's the biggest understatement in this whole story. But . . . also there was this fear. Would I . . . could I be that fortunate? I figured the odds were better for winning the lottery. Why would God all of a sudden be that good to me? I had not done anything of any considerable worth. Maybe it was the $50.00 I gave to the Shriners. Anyway, I sure wasn't going to look for long teeth in the mouth of a free horse. I was thinking of the late Martin Luther King when he said, "Free at last, free at last."

It was on a Saturday morning, sun shining, clear skies, warm temperature, and a day that makes your God look benevolent, a day for flying kites, walking in the park or riding your bike through the French Quarter. I didn't care what kind of fun I was missing; it was a good day for moving. (Not just moving anybody mind you.) I was glad to help. That way I could make sure that nothing was left behind. He would have no reason to come back.

On Sunday the sky turned black and by the next day Katrina was in full swing. My wife, who had heard about my conversation with GOD, started getting on my back for causing a hurricane. I promptly told her that we had had many hurricanes in the past and none of them had anything to do with her brother and I didn't want to hear any more nonsense down that line of thinking. As far as I was concerned her brother was gone and that was worth any hurricane. Anyway I didn't believe all that superstitious bunk.

That was Monday and on Tuesday the levees broke. He had stayed with us for the hurricane and after the levees broke his apartment was completely flooded. Yep, you guessed it, he moved back in with us. But . . . hold on . . . I'll bet you think you got the whole story. Well you don't. His job got flooded out too and they had to move to a new location that was about five miles from our new house. This last slap was enough to convince me not to harass my brother-in-law anymore.

Now I am afraid to even think about him leaving. I give up many concessions in fear that he may want to leave. I do all this because I love New Orleans and I am afraid that God will wipe it out next time.

Now the reason no names are mentioned here is because if my brother-in-law should ever figure this out he may use it as a source of coercion. Any way you don't need to know because if I decide to kick him out, I don't want the entire city of New Orleans on my back when the whole city gets destroyed again.

WHY I HATE GEORGE BUSH

Written here are reasons to hate Bush equal to any I have ever heard and better than most. I figured I could roll around in self-pity as well as, or at least equal to, and better than most people.

Right after Katrina my daughter and I were fixing up her condo. We were laying ceramic floor tile to replace the water soaked carpet that was ruined by the rain coming in through a broken pane. Because that particular area of New Orleans did not flood, the insurance company would not pay for the damages. I sent George Bush a letter about this and he did not respond. They say he owns the insurance company. The result of this non-encounter is that we had to become a do-it-yourselfer. Well, my daughter had to become a do-it-herselfer, but I read the instructions to her.

Well, I woke up one morning and walked outside to take the remnants of our labors out to the dumpster, which hadn't been picked up since the storm. Someone in city hall said that Bush told the garbage company they didn't have to pick up the "stinky stuff" because if all those people voted for Ray—Ray Naggin, then they couldn't mind "stinky stuff." Walking back to the condo I saw a bunch of red and blue lights in front of the place.

I went to the front just in time to see a police tow truck backing up to my truck. I asked the man by the truck, who was the supervisor, what was going on. I was told to speak to the policeman. I then told him that that was my truck and I jumped in the truck and drove it down the block. I returned to the scene of the crime and the policeman gave me a ticket for parking in a tow away zone. I informed him that my daughter and I had been parking there for about eight years. He told me to go and speak to the supervisor. I smelled a "George Bush" run-around.

I went to talk to the supervisor and he showed me a sign on a lamppost that said there was no parking between the hours of 8:00am and 1:30pm because president Bush was coming down that street. I told him that I did not see any sign when I parked at 8:00pm the previous evening. I was promptly told, in a voice that indicated that I was some kind of republican nut, that they could not be expected to broadcast the president's route in advance. The sign had been put up after 10:30pm.

Only someone as satanically inclined as George Bush could think up of a scheme like this; put the sign up after everyone has to be in their homes for the curfew.

After explaining that I wasn't a republican, but a tax paying, card carrying communist, he calmed down and said that the policeman wasn't allowed to tear up the ticket, but that he (the supervisor) would be at the hearing and explain the circumstances. He was sure they would dismiss the ticket.

I apologized for calling him and his mother all kinds of names and went back inside the condo when he told me how lucky I was not to be a republican.

I went down to the parking ticket court on the assigned date only to find that Katrina had flooded the place and George Bush hadn't seen fit to allocate any money to have it renovated. I began to wonder what kind of president we had. Maybe all those rumors about his insensitivity were true. Well, I sure won't vote for him again. I didn't remember voting for him last time. In fact I don't think I voted last time. Well, I sure won't vote again next time either. That'll teach 'em a lesson.

I then called the phone number on the back of the ticket and someone on the other end of the line said that I would have to go to the courthouse across the river. When I went into the courthouse, the janitor told me that I was in the wrong place because George Bush hadn't given the city any money to expand the operation of that court.

He suggested I call city hall.

What a great idea! Why hadn't I thought of that? After all, that janitor only graduated from the second grade. And here I was with a sixth grade correspondence school education. I called city hall and the lady that answered said all of the telephones were down between city hall and the various departments. She said the mayor had personally spoken to George Bush about the problem but it seems the president chose to ignore the situation. When I told a friend of mine about that he said the president probably ignored Ray-Ray because everybody else did.

After talking to that city hall rocket scientist I decided to seek another avenue of justice. I went to the city impound lot and was greeted by another patron of scholastic achievement. She could have a doctorate in personal grooming; her attire was perfect. There was only one thing wrong, she had gaudy tattoos on her hands. There was one redeeming tattoo on her arm, though. It said, "I hate George Bush."

After thoroughly explaining my problem to her she told me to wait for about 10 minutes. A half hour later she came back and said there must be some mistake because she could not find my truck anywhere on the lot. I wanted to grab her by the neck and shake some of her false teeth loose, but there were several policemen around, so I just motioned for her to follow me to the front door where I ceremoniously showed her my truck. Big mistake. She said that I should be ashamed.

She also said that I could be arrested for giving a false report. Then she said that the president didn't give the city any money for overtime and all of her time was precious. I figured that when I walked in and saw her filing her fingernails. George Bush probably bought them all fingernail files. Seemed like something he would do.

A week later I received a notice from the city that I now owed fifty dollars for not appearing on the appointed date. I promptly called the number on the letterhead and was told that it was not a working number. I wondered how long it would take Uncle W. to let the people have phones again. Maybe he should wear earplugs to keep his brains from falling out. I called city hall again and was told to go to the address on the notice and explain everything. It couldn't be that easy. No way. George must be slipping.

I was right; it wasn't that easy. They should change the name of New Orleans to the "Big Uneasy". The doorman at the building of the address said that they had moved to another building a couple of doors down the street. He said George Bush had promised that FEMA would fix the building, but the boss of Fema is George's second cousin on his brother's girlfriend's side and he does what ever he wants. And apparently he didn't want to fix up any buildings for a bunch of democrats.

I went to the indicated building and talked to the receptionist who told me that the only people that were there were the people that collected the fines and that I would have to wait until the judges returned. Well, waiting a half hour or so didn't seem too bad, after all, I had been tracking this down for two months. I told the receptionist that I wouldn't mind waiting until lunch hour was over. She said that I misunderstood what she had told me and that George Bush had the judges evacuated to Las Vegas for the storm and did not give them any money to return home. Hello, Uncle W., don't you know that there is gambling in Las Vegas and that the only thing in New Orleans that is bigger than the Saints is Harrahs Casino. How stupid can you get?

Probably the only reason he married Miss Laura is so she can remind him that he has to breathe every now and then. I was told to go home and wait for another notice.

Six months later another notice came saying that I now owed one hundred and fifty dollars for fines and penalties. I guess they needed the money to bring the judges back home. Well, I now had over a hundred dollars in bridge tolls, gasoline, parking meters and parking lots, not to say anything about my time, so I figured one more trip wouldn't break me. One thing I couldn't figure out was how George Bush got to put the tolls on the Mississippi River Bridge but I was sure that the councilman that told me that wasn't fibbing. It just fit George's character. That man is impossible, he should stick to what he was elected to do. I don't exactly know what that is, but then I am not expected to know since I am not the one elected to that office.

I went to the address on the third floor and saw a man who said he was a temp and would only be there until the real judge got out of jail. I explained my situation to him and said that I had witnesses. He said that my daughter didn't count as a witness because she would have biased testimony.

Then he told me that the parking ticket supervisor had made enough money to retire. George Bush had paid him ten dollars for every ticket he gave to a democrat. He had bought a piece of land next to the president's ranch in Crawford, Texas and had built a parking lot at the entrance to the ranch. The result was that I had no witness. How convenient was that? Thank you, George.

I then went to the fourth floor and saw a man by the name of Mr. Loo. He looked oriental and I figured him for a ChiCom because when I told him the whole story, and showed him my communist party card, he said that he would drop all penalties and just let me get away with the twenty dollars fine. I figured he must have an inside track with Uncle George to be able to do that. I agreed, paid my fine and left.

Bush does some hateful things. He was going to call his dog "Mr. Harry", but he changed his mind and named it Barney Frank after another good man in congress. And although on the face of it, it doesn't seem right, when you follow the dog around (a Scottie with his tail sticking straight up) the resemblance is remarkable. Some people in congress paid a page to put a lead weight on the dog's tail, but they had to take it off because the dog then looked like Nancy Pelosi with a bad haircut.

I hope the next president calls his dog "MR. W." That would really endear him to 95% of his constituents. Of course the new president would have to explain the connection, but I am sure that after a few months his supporters would get it.

As for me, I still hate George and the Bushes he came out of. A gooney bird in the hand is worth more than all them Bushes put together. Except Miss Laura, she's hot.

Now I told all of this to my friend, who also hates George, and I took it upon myself to include some of his comments, which I have adopted as my own.

He says he saw George's dog on television saying he would sell the family secrets. A president should have an honorable dog and that just goes to show you how stupid George Bush is. I never saw that commercial on television, but Mr. Bush must have paid a lot of money to get a dog that talks. (Probably one of them secret CIA clone dogs they use on them special black ops.)

Any way he shouldn't be advertising his bean business while he is president. Mr. Jimmy didn't advertise his peanuts and he turned out to be just as good as our first president, Damsel Washington.

And he also said that President Bush gave Florida to his brother so he could be some kind of a big shot governor and steal the election for him. Now, for me, I don't go in for that relative hiring stuff. My father-in law owns a garbage truck company and he has been trying to get me to work for him for years, but I refuse. It doesn't matter that he pays more than welfare; I still wouldn't work for a relative.

Look at Mr. Clinton, who was another good president, He was honest and stuck to his morals. He didn't hire his wife to be one of them secretaries the president has. In fact he didn't even want her to come around his office. Now that's a man who doesn't mix business with pleasure. Anyway, George should take some lessons from Mr. Bill, but he is too proud to say somebody else knows better.

Then my neighbor, Pedro, says he hates Bush also and he asked me to write down his reason, I agreed, although I already have enough reasons of my own.

He said that he used to cut the grass at the ranch in Crawford, but since he didn't have a social security card Bush had him fired. That was the reason Bush gave, but Pedro almost had enough time on the job to retire and Bush didn't want to give him a pension. Now that's mean and hateful, especially when the man won't be able to get another good job because he doesn't speak English.

And my good friend at the Sneak A Pak Arms Warehouse, Ali Babba, says Bush has his brother down in Gitmo. Now Ali may have to go out of business because his brother was the delivery truck driver. He has been in Gitmo for five years and still doesn't know what he did wrong. They told Ali that his brother was going to commit suicide. I think that's his brother's personal business and Bush shouldn't put him in prison; he should be in therapy so he can get back to driving trucks. We need drivers with a Hazmat endorsement. President Bush's insecurities are readily apparent.

I figure if that woman Any Colder, that fat guy Russian Limbo, Spawn Vanity and Bill O'Smiley can write books praising G.W., then I should make a lot of money writing about how much I hate him.

After all, there are a lot of smart people like me out there that can figure these things out. We don't need to listen to a bunch of pro-Bush biased TV guys like Grin Back who's always crying about something. Hey, we all can't be wrong. At least not when they all have good reasoning ability like me. They'll fix this country next election. We will get a president with big ears so he can hear the people.

LAGNIAPPE FROM A.

ODE TO A WORM

The lamb is most often thought
To be the meekest of our lot,
Behold the worm! He's most shy.
His meal is all that have to die.

For what besides the hand of man
Tills the soil in every land?
What squiggles with a little squirm?
That meek and mild little worm.

When men die, they feed this heir
The eternal worm is always there.
It is the worm that lies in wait.
That slimy, grimy, fishing bait.

When the bomb is dropped and man is gone
The worm is heir to his throne.
When man is toppled from his berth
The worm inherits all the earth.

THE EYES HAVE IT

Were I to be
What my friends see
I would have to be
A better me.

And to say the least
I'm not quite the beast
That's seen by those
Known as my foes.

Am I good or am I bad?
It's a question I've always had.
And all the answers are confusing
It depends on whose eyes you're using.

THE LOG

The silver ash fell from the log
And the embers glowed anew
And gave the illusion of life restored
With each slight breeze that blew.

I pondered this event with awe
That this limb should keep me warm.
Knowing such a meager death,
Yet still exuding charm.

Then I thought of fleshy things
From mouse to pachyderm.
They have a humble task in death
As dinner for the worm.

I again thought of all my sins.
My soul shall burn in hell
Forever pleasing Satan's whim
I'll stoke his fires well.

Oh! How I envy that piece of wood,
How better off would I be?
I would burn but a little while
Had I been born a tree.

SANTA CHRONICLES

By
Uncle Benton

My assistant, One Eye, and I were in Alaska near the Arctic Circle working on an all weather guidance system for aircraft. It was the perfect place for testing the systems the air force kept sending us. The weather was such that it snowed all day (the months we had day) and it snowed all night (the months we had night.) Even when there was day it was almost as dark as the night. The temperature was so far below zero we had to dig down thirty feet to get to the bottom of the thermometer to take a reading. (And then we had to thaw out the liquid in the thermometer with a blowtorch to get an accurate reading.) It was so cold that we had to put mittens on the hands of our clock to prevent it from getting frostbite.

Now being a Cajun from South Louisiana, never having seen snow and thinking it to be some big Yankee lie, I had applied for this job and got it. I later learned that only two people had applied for it and since I applied first, One Eye was my assistant. He was a pilot who had two eyes. He got his nickname because his real name was Ivan which had only one "I". His secondary job was to fly out every month and get our supplies.

We lived in a tent buried in the snow with a chimney ladder to give us access to the outside world. Another tent was buried in the snow to house our generators with the same kind of access.

One day we heard a big commotion in the generator tent and One Eye went to investigate. A polar bear had fallen down the chimney. One eye and the polar bear had a fight and the bear scratched out one of One Eye's eyes. His wife called the insurance company to collect the insurance and they wrote back that they were not responsible if he wanted to change his name to Van. It took a lot of explaining, but they finally realized that he had lost an eye and not an "I".

A year later, on a supply run, he made a turn to his blind side and crashed into a mountain. His wife collected the insurance money and asked me if I knew of any other one-eyed pilots. She was looking for a new husband.

This story starts about six months before One Eye died.

One Christmas Eve day or maybe Christmas Eve night, depending on your definition of day and night, outside of our igloo workshop we heard such a clatter. We ran outside to see what was the matter. There was a sleigh with eight tiny reindeer and we knew it was St. Nick.

Santa told us that his reindeer could not see in the terrible weather we were having and wanted us to put him up for the night. Well, that meant Christmas would have to be cancelled and we could have none of that. Mais, non, Podnuh!! (Cajun for the modern way of saying "No way, Jose.")

My assistant and I brought out Rudy, one of our most trusted sled dogs, strapped an all weather antenna on his head and fitted his snout with a red indicator light that glowed as long as he was on a course set by the driver. It was the latest model of an all—weather radar. Santa tied him to the front of his team, thanked us and drove off.

The next day (or night) Santa paid us a visit and thanked us. He said everything had worked perfectly except that people mistook our sled dog for a reindeer and even started calling the dog "Rudolph". One cowboy had made up a song about him. We all had a good laugh about that. He also started telling us about some of the gifts he had given.

He was a regular visitor after that Christmas and after One Eye died he would stay with me for a while. He said that since the days were so long he could stay and not be missed. We had hot chocolate and he told me many more tales.

The old weather station has long been closed, but Santa still comes to my house near the bayou after he finishes his rounds. He has acquired a taste for our Louisiana gumbo. One time he showed up with eight alligators and one red-eyed crocodile pulling a pirogue. The crocodile was named Raoul and his big red eyes were like Superman's x-ray vision.

Santa needed Raoul because it was really foggy on the bayous and he said Louisiana is the only place he could have a real Cajun Christmas.

Now, I am not given to stretching the truth, and Santa is known for never telling a lie, so written in the following pages are his tales to the best of my recollection. Here are the adventures of Santa Claus as told by Santa to Uncle Benton.

But first a tribute to Raoul. Some Cajun wrote a song.

RAOUL THE RED-EYED REPTILE

Raoul the red-eyed reptile
Had really bright red eyes
And if you ever saw them
You would even swear he cries.

All of the other gators
Would make such fun of him.
They wouldn't play with Raoul
So he taught himself to swim.

Then one Cajun Christmas Eve,
Bayous full of fog,
Santa asked Red-eyed Raoul
Will you guide my big pirogue.

When all of the Cajuns saw him
They shouted out, "Yahoo."
Raoul the red-eyed reptile
We will all remember you.

* CHRISTMAS DAY *

*S*anta was dashing through the snow
Above the ground about a mile or so
Just cruising around to here and there
Heading for, he knew not where.

*W*hen far away down below
He saw some people moving slow.
He turned the sleigh around
And eased the reindeer near the ground.

*T*hree men, there were, each with a gift
And could Santa please give them a lift.
Their camels, it seems, were all wore out
From carrying these gifts all about.

*T*hey didn't know just how far
They'd have to go to catch that star.
Santa had room in the sleigh
And in a flash they were away.

*I*n the wink of an eye they were at a manger
Looking down on the newborn stranger.
While the men brought gifts for the babe
Santa was talking with the angel Gabe.

*S*anta said, and Gabe agreed,
That this idea was great indeed.
And with Santa's knowledge of navigation
He could visit every nation

*A*nd with his elves making toys
He'd bring real joy to girls and boys.
And with his sleigh at the speed of light
He could do it all in just one night.

*S*anta bid them all good-bye
And as he shot up into the sky
They all heard him say,
"I think I'll call it *"Christmas Day."*

SANTA'S OLIVE

The Christmas skies were nearly clear
When Santa landed on the pier.
He saw the sailor near the ship
Who was the purpose for this trip.

This was Popeye's lucky day
Olive Oyle stepped from the sleigh.
And in her outstretched hands
She had a case of spinach cans.

Love was blooming on that night
As Santa sped out of sight.
He knew their future was right on track
He tied up Bluto in his sack

SANTA CLAUS WATER COMPANY

Santa's sleigh went down the hill
To meet up with Jack and Jill.
He dug down deep in his sack.
Padding for Jill, aspirins for Jack.

And an HMO for they were prone
To fall and tumble and break a bone.
And just because he thought he oughta,
A brand new pail for fetching water.

SANTA AND BIG BEN

Santa gave a kite to a man one night
With a string tied to it.
It was a wire string
With a key on a ring
And soon after, Frankly, Ben flew it.

MARY CHRISTMAS

Mary had a little lamb, but that was long ago
That was long before her hair had turned white as snow.
That was yesterday when she was very young.
Was it yesterday when the school bells rung?

This was her first Noel all alone,
Her spouse had died, he was gone.
She ran to the window as she heard a noise
And saw Santa with his bag of toys.

She reached for the door and opened it wide
Just as Santa jumped inside.
He shuffled his sack and dug real deep
And woke the lamb that had been asleep.

"Buddy is his name, he's yours to keep
He came from my own flock of sheep."
Then he added, with a HO or two,
"A gift for you from my ewe."

OLD MAC SANTA

Santa drove through the Christmas storm
And stopped at old Mac Donald's farm
Out of his sack he took
A first grade spelling book.

He looked at old Mac Donald's letter
And said, "You need to spell a little better."
"The vowels are not EIEIO,
It's AEIOU, as the book will show.

"EIEIO." repeated Mr. Mac.
Santa laughed as he grabbed his sack.
"I know the problem now." He said.
"Next year you'll get a hearing aid."

WHAT BUGS SANTA CLAUS

Santa Claus stopped at Elmer's house.
He knew Mr. Fudd had no spouse
And his only really bad habit
Was hunting that "Doggone Wabbit."

Under the tree he put a new gun
And a box of bullets just for fun.
He left the house with a great big grin
Cause he knew Mr. Fudd could not win.

When he finished his round
He came back through town.
He laughed at what he thought so funny.
He saw old Fudd chasing the bunny.

He paused watching the race
It was one heck of a chase.
Bugs looked up and said, "Thanks.
The bullets you left were only blanks."

SANTA'S ROCK AND ROLL

It was one foggy Christmas night
With no known landmarks in sight,
But Santa found Tupelo
In spite of fog and snow.

The young man's letter was quite clear
As to what he wanted this year.
He only wanted a new guitar
So he could become a star.

But Santa knew he needed more
To make the crowds clap and roar.
When Elvis appeared in low ground fog
Santa gave him an Old Hound Dog.

ABBOTT AND COSTELLO MEET SAINT NICK

It was a rare night in Hollywood
The skies were clear and the air smelled good.
Santa had made his stops and was nearly through,
Just one more stop for an actor named Lou.

Lou was short and round and full of humor
And Santa had heard of the latest rumor
That he and Lou were the closest kin
And that Lou might even be his twin.

Lou had written a letter
Requesting a real go-getter.
His act was starting to fail
As his jokes were getting way too stale.

Santa was able to comply.
In his bag he had a guy
That he knew for a fact
Could beef up any act.

Lou was waiting at the gate
As Santa stopped his eight.
As filling requests was his habit
He introduced Lou to Mr. Abbott.

As Santa jumped into his sleigh
They both heard him say,
"To make your dreams come true.
Lou, this Bud's for you."

CHRISTMAS IS A RAT RACE

'Twas Christmas Eve and all through the house
Thomas was searching for any old mouse.
But not a creature was stirring, not even a scent
And he was wondering where they all went.

When a clatter he heard out on the grass
He ran to the window and looked through the glass.
He saw Santa grab a sack from the back of his seat
And jump to the roof (In itself a mighty feat.)

He came down the chimney in a little red suit
Which was now black from all of the soot.
He drank a little coffee and ate all the pie
And turned to the tree with a twinkling eye.

He went to his work as quiet as a mouse.
Under the tree he put a small house
Wrapped in a ribbon with a small tag.
Then he turned and closed up his bag.

As he left through the big patio door.
He said, "Through the chimney no more."
He jumped in his sleigh and shot to the sky.
He yelled, "Merry Christmas Tom, here's mud in your eye."

He made one more pass over the house
And saw Thomas chasing the mouse.
Santa knew this year would be merry.
The tag had said, "A mouse named Jerry."

SANTA AND THE WOLF

The big bad wolf was coughing and wheezing
His throat was sore and he was always sneezing.
This Christmas would be bad, really tough
Because he wasn't able to huff and puff.

That's when Santa brought him a cup
Filled with medicine to fix him up.
To Santa the wolf was no stranger,
He knew the pigs would be in danger.

So Santa dropped from his sleigh
To the first pig, a bale of hay.
To the second a bundle of sticks,
And to the third a ton of bricks.

When at last he finished his round
He detoured back through Piggy Town.
He saw the hay house smattered
And the stick house was scattered.

Then he saw in the brick house yard
The big bad wolf blowing hard.
Then Santa continued homeward bound
Knowing the pigs were safe and sound.

SANTA GOES HOLLYWOOD

The L.A. skies were filled with stars
The roads below were jammed with cars.
So Santa flew above the ground
No traffic signs to slow him down.

He had been here years ago
To help the man put on a show.
He now asked Santa in a letter
To make the show a little better.

Walt had a mouse named Steamboat Willie
Santa thought the name quite silly
Knowing movie fans to be quite picky
Santa brought a mouse named Mickey.

He also brought a master plan
And a deed to a lot of land.
Santa said as he shook Walt's hand,
"Now go and build your Disneyland."

SANTA AND THE FARM HOUSE MOUSE

Santa parked his big red ride
Near the barn and went inside.
There he found three blind mice
And gave them something very nice.

Much to the three's surprise
He gave them contacts for their eyes.
And then to make them feel anew
He stuck their tails back on with glue.

He went to the house and found
The farmer and wife sleeping sound.
Santa knew what she could use.
He left her some tennis shoes.

He turned to leave and then he thought
He'd better leave the knife he'd brought.
But not to harm limb or life
It was a rubber carving knife.

SANTA'S EGG

'Twas Christmas Eve morning and all was ready.
The elves were holding the reindeer real steady
Because the deer all knew it was their day
And they were all anxious to be on the way.

Santa ran to the phone when he heard it ring
And he heard the voice of his majesty the king.
Through weeping and sobbing he heard the king say
That Humpty Dumpty was the cause of dismay.

Santa knew Humpty from the year before
When he had left him at the castle door.
Humpty was the best of eggs, or as good as any.
And Santa knew because he had seen so many.

And now he learned from the call
That Humpty Dumpty had a great fall
And from the sound of things, he could tell
That Humpty had broken his shell.

He assured the king that all would be well
Especially if Humpty had broken his shell.
He said he would be there later today
And he packed something special in his sleigh.

Santa got to the castle early that night.
The king's men and their horses were such a sight
All scurrying and jumping and running around,
But Santa's arrival calmed them all down.

He told them to build a big fire "If you please."
Then he pulled from his sack some ham and cheese
And a huge, gigantic, great big frying pan
And said, "There will be an omelet for every man."

And to the king who was feeling blue,
"A friend of mine sends a gift for you."
He opened the sack near his leg
And gave the king an Easter egg.

SANTA BEARS THE LOAD

Homeward bound and flying low
Santa had one more stop to go.
He was looking for his little friend
Who would be waiting 'round the bend.

His little friend who lived alone
Had called him on the telephone
And asked if Santa knew
Someone who was lonely too.

And would Santa bring him on Christmas Day
To see if he would like to stay.
Santa had someone in mind
A creature real true and kind.

Santa landed on the ground
Near Piglet jumping up and down.
Santa said, "Hey, you there,
Here's your friend, Pooh the Bear."

They all talked for awhile
Then Santa said with a smile,
"Next year when you're a little bigger
I'll bring you a cat by the name of Tigger."

SANTA'S BAKERY

Santa had made a stop
At the local bakery shop
He bought a pie
And shot to the sky.

And quick as a wink he was there
A place named for Pooh the Bear.
It was at this corner
He saw little Jack Horner.

He had a present for Jack,
Which he took from his sack.
With a twinkle in his eye
Jack took the peach pie.

Now Jack was not dumb
But he thought it was plum.
Santa said nothing to spoil the joy
Of a four year old little boy.

SANTA AIRLINE

Santa had no concern
That the boys he chose could learn
Because he knew since time began
That flight was part of every man.

And he was glad to be a part
Of the plan that would be the start
And none better to be found
To help them get off the ground.

So it was one Christmas night
He gave to Willie and Orville Wright
Two kits for making model planes
And thoughts of moon dust in their veins.

He knew these boys would soon be grown
And make bigger models of their own.
But until then, in their hands
He placed a box of rubber bands.

SANTA'S JUMPER

Santa would always read his mail
Before he hit the Christmas trail.
It was easier to remember
If he read it in December.

A letter from Jumping Jack Jeep,
Famed for his candlestick leap,
Wanted Santa to tell
Of a magical spell.

He heard the rumor that Santa's tune
Had helped the cow jump over the moon
And at the Olympic games next year
He wanted to jump like a deer.

Now J.J. was nimble and J.J. was quick,
But his highest jump was the candlestick
Santa thought, "It's magic he'll get,
But he won't be jumping and that's a bet."

"When I get there we'll have a talk
I'll have him climbing up a stalk."
And with that settled he told the elf,
"Get magic beans from the shelf."

SANTA'S LISA

Italy was Santa's last stop that year.
He had a special note from here.
His friend had a problem Santa could fix
If he came over with his bag of tricks.

A friend of a friend whose husband had died
Never laughed, only sat and cried.
She was a pretty girl, but always whining
Never seeing the silver lining.

So Santa entered the studio
And said hello to Leonardo.
Then he saw the lady he had
Been told about looking so sad.

Santa gave her a rose with grace
And a smile broke out on Lisa's face.
"Painta her nowa, Leonaarrdo."
Santa said. "Nowa I musta go."

SUPER SANTA

Santa stopped at the house of Kent
In response to a letter Pa Kent had sent.
That little Clark would soon be grown
And striking out on his own.

And Clark would be fighting crime
So right now would be the time
To fix him up with a vest
To make bullets bounce off his chest.

Santa left Clark some boots for speed
And the cape to fly, that he'd need.
And in case the bad guys shoot
He left him a blue bulletproof suit.

As Santa got into his sleigh
He heard Pa Kent say,
"Come back, Santa, when you can.
You really are a super man."

SANTA'S CHERRY TREE

Santa thought the night was fairly warm
As he stopped at the Washington farm.
The axe requested was much too large
So he brought a hatchet for young George.

And now I'll tell you the reason why
Young George could not tell a lie.
Santa had looked in his crystal ball
And saw the tree that would fall.

And Santa, being so very wise,
Did not like children telling lies.
To George's dad, whom he had much respect for,
He gave a machine called a lie detector.

SANTA'S WATCH

Hickory and Dickory lived in a small house
With a doctor, who was a small mouse.
Hickory was called Hickey, and Dickory, Dickey
And doc's real name was plain old Mickey

It was Doc's letter that Santa got
Saying he never wanted a lot,
But his friends were always late,
Never on time for a date.

Some timely advice
And a clock for the mice
And it would do no harm
If it had an alarm.

There were no small clocks that day
So Santa loaded his sleigh
With a grandfather clock
He had in his stock.

Christmas morning brought great surprise
When the mice opened their eyes
And saw the timepiece in the hall.
They wasted no time at all.

They ran up the clock for fun
And the clock struck one
The other one helped him down the clock
Where he was patched up by the Doc.

And that's what made Doc decide
To be called Mickey and take a ride
With Santa if he could
And meet Disney in Hollywood.

SANTA AND THE TALL MAN

Santa's sleigh was void of toys
But he had one more stop in Illinois.
It was at New Salem General Store
The man was waiting in the door.

The man was tall and lanky, really thin
A friendly voice asking Santa in.
He had asked Santa for a portable gym
As he was embarrassed by being so slim.

Santa said, knowing what was best
And ignoring the man's request,
"Here's a law book for you to read.
Honest, Abe, this you'll need."

SANTA WILL TELL

Traveling over Europe one year
Bringing his usual Christmas cheer
Santa saw the man below
Who wanted a sight for his bow.

No such sight had yet been made.
At least not one fit for the trade.
So the bowman got instead
A great big pumpkin painted red.

Bigger than an apple and looked liked one
It was a gift for the bowman's son.
And just to improve the view
He gave Mr. Tell eyeglasses too.

SANTA IS BACK IN IRAQ

A camel came in 2002
With a letter from you know who.
Santa was astonished, taken aback
To get a request from this man in Iraq.

About thirty years before
He kicked Santa out the door
And his reasons were well cloaked
When Santa's visa was revoked.

It was obvious from the blank check
This man wasn't playing with a full deck.
He wanted to buy a missile defense
Santa just laughed at such nonsense.

Came Christmas night in Iraq
Every child knew Santa was back.
He gave a brand new toy
To every girl and every boy.

He made the palace his last stop
To see the man at the top.
Question: "Did you bring what I need?"
Answer: "OH yes, Oh yes, Oh yes indeed!"

Santa gave the man a travel kit
With a map to a cave in it,
And just to close the loops,
He gave one to the troops.

Santa dropped leaflets from his sleigh
Telling the children of a brand new day
And he'd be coming back from now on
Because Saddam Hussein would soon be gone.

SANTA SMELLS A RAT

Santa stopped at the village of Pied
Where the piper there had just died.
The increased population of rats
Had scared off all of the cats.

The people would not go out
With the rats all about.
They asked Santa for relief.
Santa always rewarded belief.

He brought an iron box
And filled it with blocks
Of good old Wisconsin Cheddar
Tasted great, but smelled even better.

The rats could not wait
To get at the bait
And the trap worked with ease.
"Ah, the power of cheese!"

SANTA'S 2 PLUS 2

A letter came to Santa one night
Traveling at the speed of light.
It was a simple request, easy to fill
But it was passe, over the hill.

The man was working on equations in math.
His blackboard was the source of his wrath
Because his equations, however so small
Would go over the edge onto the wall.

He wanted a blackboard from here to there
So he would always have room to spare.
Now there was no blackboard as big as all that
And blackboards for scientist were just old hat.

Santa parked his sleigh on a big snow bank
Near the lab of Einstein, Albert, not Frank.
"Here's your computer it works real well."
Santa said, "Dude, you're getting a Dell!"

SANTA AND MARIA

In 1491 as Santa was preparing to go
A polar bear came out of the snow
With a letter from an Italian chap
Wanting the latest world map.

This fellow had the notion
He could sail west on the ocean
And reach the lands of the east
And save months of travel at least.

Santa, having long since found
That the world was really round,
Left Chris a map for the great quest
And a compass that only pointed west.

Now "Maria" was Columbus's ship
But before he made the famous trip
They all heard him exclaim,
"I'll make Santa her first name!"

SANTA AND SPIDEY

Santa saw, when he opened up the letter,
That it was signed by a real pace setter
Who was led to understand
That Santa would lend a hand.

He was calling on Santa because
Santa knew everyone that ever was.
He had a special company to run
And it would take a special someone.

To build up a network from the inside
And download data worldwide.
Santa then sat down and wrote
Young Peter Parker a nice little note.

He asked Peter to come up with a design
For a worldwide network line.
After all there is nobody who can
Design a web like Spiderman.

SANTA'S OTHER NAME

A letter came in one day
From a lady named Hathaway.
Her boyfriend was a ne'er do well
As far as she could tell.

Santa knew well of whom she spoke
A penniless, but intelligent sort of bloke.
One who spent his midsummer night's dreams
On ploys and plays and plots and schemes.

Along with the letter that day
Came Shakespeare's latest play,
With the request for a private reading
To determine what it was needing.

Roseanne and Julio, the names were strange
And that was Santa's biggest change.
Romeo and Juliet they soon became
A rose much sweeter by another name.

And then, to make matters worse
There was no rhyme in any verse
So Christmas night Santa gave to him
A book called "Homonym, antonym and Synonym."

SANTA'S MAIL BAG

Santa gets enough letters and cards
To fill a thousand back yards.
So Santa was recycling a long time ago.
Before it was cool to be doing so.

But the elves could only handle so much
And when the volume had grown to such
That it required more than 24 hours a day,
Santa had to find another way.

So now every pop and mom
Logs on to santa@aol.com
And now you hear the PC wail
"Santa, you've got mail."

SANTA AND BRUCIE BABY

One correspondence came in an unusual manner
It came as a signal from Bruce Wayne's manor.
Alfred, the sender, said that
He only wanted a baseball bat.

Mr. Wayne thought his plan,
As he was a Yankee fan,
To fight crime in the disguise
Of a batboy to be wise.

Santa didn't send Alfred the bat
At least not the bat that
Is used in baseball.
Oh, no not at all!

Never send a batboy to do
A Batman's job for you.
Santa left on the batcave wall
A photo of Dracula, costume and all.

SANTA BASEBALL

One time Santa read
A letter written in red
From a man that was dead,
Or so the letter said.

The man wanted a reference
For his son to have preference
To a job on a baseball team.
As this was his only dream.

Now Count Dracula was very explicit
His son wanted nothing illicit.
He would be the best worker on Earth
Since he was a batboy by birth.

SANTA'S TEDDY

Polar mail comes year round
Neither sleet nor snow can slow it down
Nor dark of night at high noon.
Neither hurricane, tornado nor typhoon.

In came a letter from President Teddy
Saying that he was almost ready.
To move heaven and earth over there,
But he didn't say where.

Teddy would put America's might
If Santa would locate the site
Because Santa knew every Isthmus
Traveling the world every Christmas.

A canal to be dug, one so gigantic
It would join the Pacific to the Atlantic.
So the biggest ships could pass through
Saving time and money too.

Santa knew without a doubt
Panama was the place to pick out.
And the mountain trees would lace
The huge canal with such grace.

All the noise Teddy could make
Would not make heaven shake
And even his big stick
Would not do the trick.

But for all he was worth
Teddy could move some earth
So along with a map drawn to scale
Santa gave him a shovel and pail.

SANTA AND HIS ELVES R SMART

You know that old lady who lived in a shoe
Who had so many kids she knew not what to do
And you also know Santa is gentle and kind
But all those kids put him in a bind.

He would have to put so much stuff in his sleigh
He couldn't haul it all in one day.
So he gave them some coupons and a big blue bus
And told them to go to "TOYS R US."

SANTA'S BARNYARD

About the cow that jumped over the moon
When it heard Santa's magic tune.
Well what goes up must come down
And it was heading toward the ground.

When Henny Penny saw it falling
"The sky is falling," she ran around calling.
It turned out to be a false alarm
And they both went to Santa's farm.

They became the best of friends
But that is not where it ends.
Santa gave them a TV contract so
They could star in the "Cow and Chicken" show

SANTA CUTS NO CORNERS

The letters from Hollywood are usually strange
They're mostly about making a change.
A new star for this movie or a line for that play
And somehow Santa would always save the day.

Santa was the master when it was pertaining
To the real art of entertaining
He knew what kids liked to see and hear
Because they sent him letters every year.

The producer sent Santa a wire
Looking for someone special to hire.
"Cut no corners," said the boss.
"We'll soak up any loss."

Cartoons specials were a high form of art
And Santa gave many their very first start.
So now Mr. Crabbie would have a fair chance
He and his pal "Sponge Bob Square Pants."

SANTA AND POLAR

Papa Bear sent word to cousin Polar Bear
Relating some trouble in the forest there
And Polar told Santa Exaggerating a bit,
But Santa got the gist of it.

Goldie Locks had broken a chair
Belonging to one Baby Bear.
Now Santa couldn't be wrong
His elves made that chair pretty strong.

Santa decided to make another chair
Strong enough for Polar Bear.
But that's not what worried him
So he packed equipment for a gym.

He gave a treadmill in a big pink box
And a diet book to Goldie Locks.
And a note that said, "Please don't wait.
It's time for you to lose some weight.

SANTA KNOWS THE WOLF

The Big Bad Wolf writes every year
And Santa always lends an ear
'Cause the things Wolf wants, like as not,
Will be involved in a naughty plot.

Now this request came the year before
Wolf was huffing and puffing at the piggy's door.
He wanted rabbit ears so he could get
A better picture on the TV set.

He wanted bigger glasses for his eyes
'Cause the TV set was small in size.
Santa knew what Wolf had in mind
And also knew it would not be kind.

Santa also knew Red Riding Hood
And thought the kid was very good.
He wouldn't like to see her hurt
By Wolf in Granny's undershirt.

So he left big deaf ears under the tree
And fake eyeglasses so Wolf couldn't see.
And he left some big false teeth too
Shut up tight with superglue.

SANTA WHERE ARE YOU?

A letter came from the S.P.C.A.
About a man from Big L.A.
Who, poor man, must have been stricken
With something or other, He wanted a chicken.

Now the only Chicken Santa knew
Was with Cow in a cartoon revue.
Santa was puzzled, but not for long
He knew in L.A. he couldn't go wrong

Out there they had twists and turns in every plot
Irony was treasured on the studio lot.
He had a dog that was scared of the dark
In fact, even afraid of its very own bark.

The dog was chicken without any doubt,
But at the end of the day the dog would win out.
So under the tree, on Christmas night,
He left the dog and a little night-light.

Before he left he sat down and wrote
To Shaggy man a little note.
"The dog's name is up to you.
What do you think, will Scooby do?"

OLD MAN SANTA

It was Christmas morning when he reached the Pole
Feeling awfully tired and really cold.
The little elves unhitched the sleigh
And gave the reindeer some fresh hay.

Santa, slightly bent, went inside
And sat down near the fireside.
Retirement thoughts came to mind.
Leave this cold North Pole behind.

Bossing elves was quite a chore
Daily for three sixty-four.
And when the deer got sick
The only vet was Old St. Nick.

Then he thought of all the cheer
He brought the children every year.
After a nap he felt anew
Dismissing thoughts of being through.

Merry Christmas to all and to all a goodnight.
Although here at the pole with no sun in sight
It is hard to tell what to say
Maybe goodnight or maybe good day.

'TWAS THE DAY AFTER CHRISTMAS

'Twas the day after Christmas and all through the house
Not a creature was stirring, except Candy, Santa's sweet spouse.
The elves had packed their trunks with care
Hoping that TACA would soon be there.

The elves were all nestled all snug in their beds
While visions of CANCUN danced in their heads.
Each reindeer wearing it's own heated wrap
Was settled in the barn for a well-deserved nap.

The elves woke up to the sound of a clatter
But it was only Candy dropping a platter.
So they stayed up talking some trash,
And counting their Mexican Peso cash.

Now to their wondering ears what should they hear?
The roar of an airplane coming near.
The TACA pilot landed safely on ice so slick
The elves thought for a moment that it might be St. Nick.

The pilot appeared as the elves they came
He knew them all and called them by name.
"Hey, Patrick! Hey, Skyler! Hey Sharon! Hey, Jamie!
Hey, Tee Sid, Hannah, Brian and Amy!
Come on, Big Neal! Heidi, Brooke and Paul!
Come on, Kyle, Heyden and Ashley! Hurry up all!

Before the plane took off, and could vanish
Candy said, practicing her Spanish,
"Adios muchachos, mis amigitos
A todos buenos noches Y buenos noches a todos."

My favorite poem of all time . . . A.
The Cremation of Sam McGee
ROBERT W. SERVICE 1907

There are strange things done in the midnight sun
By the men who moil for gold
The Arctic trails have their secret tales
That would make your blood run cold;
The Northern Lights have seen queer sights,
But the queerest they ever did see
Was that night on the marge of Lake Lebarge
I cremated Sam McGee

Now Sam McGee was from Tennessee, where the cotton blooms and blows.
Why he left his home in the South to roam 'round the Pole, God only
knows.
He was always cold, but the land of gold seemed to hold him like a spell;
Though he'd often say in his homely way that "he'd sooner live in hell."

On a Christmas Day we were mushing our way over the Dawson trail.
Talk of your cold! Through the parka's fold it stabbed like a driven nail.
If our eyes we'd close, then the lashes froze till sometimes we couldn't see;
It wasn't much fun, but the only one to whimper was Sam McGee.

And that very night, as we lay packed tight in our robes beneath the snow,
And the dogs were fed, and the stars o'erhead were dancing heel to toe,
He turned to me, and "Cap," says he, "I'll cash in this trip, I guess;
And if I do, I'm asking that you won't refuse my last request."

Well, he seemed so low that I couldn't say no; then he says with a sort of
moan:
"It's the cursed cold, and it's got right hold till I'm chilled clean through
the bone.
Yet 'taint being dead—it's my awful dread of the icy grave that pains;
So I want you to swear that, foul or fair, you'll cremate my last remains."

A pal's last need is a thing to heed, so I swore I would not fail.
And we started on at the streak of dawn; but God! he looked ghastly pale.

He crouched on the sleigh and he raved all day of his home in Tennessee.
And before nightfall a corpse was all that was left of Sam McGee.

There wasn't breath in that land of death, and I hurried, horror-driven,
With a corpse half hid that I couldn't get rid, because of a promise given;
It was lashed to the sleigh, and it seemed to say: "you may tax your brawn
and brains,
But you promised true, and it's up to you to cremate those last remains."

Now a promise made is a debt unpaid, and the trail has its own stern code.
In the days to come, though my lips were dumb, in my heart how I cursed
the load.
In the long, long night, by the firelight, while the huskies, round in a ring,
Howled out their woes to the homeless snows—O God! How I loathed
the thing.

And every day that quiet clay seemed to heavy and heavier grow;
And on I went, though the dogs were spent and the grub was getting low;
The trail was bad, and I felt half mad, but I swore I would not give in;
And I'd often sing to the hateful thing, and it hearkened with a grin.

Till I came to the marge of Lake Lebarge, and a derelict there lay;
It was jammed in the ice, but I saw in a trice it was called the "Alice May."
And looked at it, and I thought a bit, and looked at my frozen chum;
Then "Here," said I, with a sudden cry, "is my crema-tor-eum."

Some planks I tore from the cabin floor, and I lit the boiler fire;
Some coal I found that was lying around, and heaped the fuel higher;
The flames just soared, and the furnace roared—such a blaze you seldom see;
And I burrowed a hole in the glowing coal, and I stuffed in Sam McGee.

Then I made a hike, for I didn't like to hear him sizzle so;
And the heavens scowled, and the huskies howled, and the wind began to
blow.
It was icy cold, but the hot sweat rolled down my cheeks, and I don't
know why;
And the greasy smoke in an inky cloak went streaking down the sky.

I do not know how long in the snow I wrestled with grisly fear;

But the stars came out and they danced about ere again I ventured near;
I was sick with dread, but I bravely said: "I'll just take a peep inside.
I guess he's cooked, and it's time I looked;" . . . then the door opened wide.

And there sat Sam, looking cool and calm, in the heart of the furnace roar;
And he wore a smile you could see for a mile, and he said: "Please close the
door.
It's fine in here, but I greatly fear you'll let in the cold and storm—
Since I left Plumtree, down in Tennessee, it's the first time I've been
warm."

There are strange things done in the midnight sun
By the men who moil for gold
The Arctic trails have their secret tales
That would make your blood run cold;
The Northern Lights have seen queer sights,
But the queerest they ever did see
Was that night on the marge of Lake Lebarge
I cremated Sam McGee

SAM McGEE
THE CURSE OF THE ALICE MAY
By A. Benton Phillips

When I was 10 years old my brother read Sam McGee to me. I didn't remember a lot of the words but the rhyme scheme and the story stayed with me for all these years. I ran across the poem last year and became absorbed in the simple complexity all over again.

And then I remembered the question I had asked my brother over 60 years ago. What happened to Sam McGee once he was thawed out? I thought it strange that this magnificent poem in its perfection gave me no closure; I guess I was too young to understand irony so I had to answer my own question.

I bow to the genius of Mr. Service and humbly offer a closure to his great work . . . . A.

EPISODE TWO

I said with a shout, "You're all thawed out!" And he gave me a great big
grin.
Then he pointed through the door to the cabin floor where the planks
had been.
I saw what must be tons of dust spilling from bags beneath the floor.
In a nearby bed a man lay dead, in his hand was an old forty-four.

We didn't dare nor did we care to ponder the when, where or why.
We just knew that for us two there was more than enough of that pie.
Sam said with a laugh, "We'll each take half and I'll be satisfied.
With all this gold, I'll leave this cold where I almost died."

We split the load and hit the road after setting the wreck on fire
From miles away we saw the Alice May now just a funeral pyre.
We headed away from the pole that day and continued through the
night
O'er fifty miles we went and the dogs were spent; the fire was still in
sight.

We traveled on 'til the snow was gone and the dogs were almost dead.

We looked back to check on that fabulous wreck from which we so
hurriedly fled.
We had not run out of the midnight sun and the stars were sparkling eyes.
A faint pink glow on the horizon snow was all that marked the May's demise.

We mushed on through 'til the warm winds blew, then we sent the dogs
back home.
We bought passage on a freighter and an hour later were heading away
from Nome
And soon forgot about not being hot the farther south we sailed.
In fact we were glad, but the crew was mad, when the cool winds failed.

The cruise was long and we both grew strong with each passing day
And now had time to wonder, to query and ponder the fate of the Alice
May.
Did that old dead man have a sort of plan and why did he hide the gold?
Why had he died, was it suicide because of the cursed cold?

Though we pondered not on this sorry lot at that opportune time
Sam could now recall the death like pall at the scene of the crime.
Sam was happy to be warm and frost free, but there was somber in the air
Every detail and clue through minute review left the mystery hanging there.

It now bothered Sam, but like a dam, he kept it all inside
He hid it well, but I could always tell he was taking it all in stride.
He says to me, "Cap," says he, "I think I have no regret.
But the Alice May could someday be the death of me yet."

We hit San Francisco Bay early in May; the weather was nice and warm.
Sam and I could feel the roulette wheel; it beckoned like a charm.
We went ashore, not too poor, each with a big bag of gold
And stopped at "Alice of the Golden Palace" "anything bought and sold."

We had women and wine, a place to dine and a place to lay the head.
Sam got drunk as a lunatic skunk and Alice put him to bed.
She stole his gold and ever so bold she set the house on fire.
She was shocked, the door was locked and the flames grew even higher.

She banged with fear, but none could hear over Sam sizzling so.

I thought for a while I could see him smile for the lack of icy snow.
The only thing found lying on the ground was a bag of melted gold
And I got relief from the belief that Sam would never again be cold.

The building burned down, right down to the ground, maybe a little below.
And in that trash and mountain of ash, a sign was put up for show,
"Here lies Alice of the Golden Palace may she finally rest in peace."
I saw the word Alice and the word after palace, will wonders never cease.

I thought of the gold and the awful cold and remembered Sam McGee
And on the marge of Lake Lebarge where the fire had set him free.
To mark my loss I made a cross with a few words and R.I.P
"Once frost bitten now fire smitten here stays Sam McGee."

There are strange things done in the midnight sun by the men who moil
for gold,
But none as strange as when fortunes change due to women whose
hearts run cold
The arctic trails may have their tales, but the loads they seldom bear
Is the ironic fate of the small and great because Death gets his share.
And the Northern Lights had no rights, as we can plainly see
Over the death or the breath of that whimpering Sam McGee

EPISODE 3
REBIRTH OF SAM McGee

After Sam's demise, much to my surprise, I rebuilt the Golden Palace.
I paid for it all with the haul we took from the shipwrecked Alice.
It was a grandiose place with a brand new face called "The Sam McGee"
There were games of chance, a place to dance, really fancy-free.

It became too much for anyone such as I to work it all.
So from way back home, just south of Nome, came the answer to my call.
My sister Joanne, could outwork a man, had a heart made of gold
And would not be shaken, when she would rake in the excess of wealth
untold.

She could be tender with any big spender and mean with those who
would cheat.
She was honest and fair and gave a good share to beggars on the street.
The place grew in fame as did the name, and so did she.
Joanne was host on the Barbary Coast, the toast of "The Sam McGee."

As beauty goes, she was the rose and none else could compare.
Well over five feet, straight white teeth, blue eyes and golden hair.
Big in the right place and small in the waist, a goddess here on earth.
She drew the crowd large and loud adding to Sam's rebirth.

Then came the day I sent her away to search in Tennessee
For the family there that would get a share of the place called "The Sam
McGee."
Down in Plumtree she found Kelly McGee, Sam's younger brother
And a little old lady by the name of Sadie, Sam's sainted mother.

Kelly was tall and as strong as the day was long (In the land of the
midnight sun.)
He was quite a guy, real handsome and shy, loved by everyone.
Miss Joanne saw in a trice, with out any advice, this was to be her man.
It was the love on her part that got to his heart; he was in love with Miss
Joanne.

It was very soon, on the third of June, she became Mrs. McGee.
And not long after, amid song and laughter, they took leave of
Tennessee.
They went to the coast to make the most of their fortune around the Bay.
It was a day to remember in mid December being received in such a way.

The band was playing, the politicians saying, "Welcome home Joanne."
The ramblers were walking; gamblers were talking about the lucky man.
Miss Joanne had said that her homestead was a little south of Nome.
Would he handle the cold for all that gold or make the Bay his home?

It became obvious to all there was a greater call that would change her mind
It was in her belly, sired by Kelly, it was holding two of a kind.
When a boy and a girl came out, there was no doubt what their names
would be.
Alice May was one; as for the son he was called Sam McGee.

There are strange things done in the midnight sun, but are soon set straight.
For none can cheat nor hope to defeat a king by the name of fate.
Nor can they stay for even a day what is slated to be.
If you think for a minute that fate is not in it, just ask young Sam
McGee.

HAIKU REASONS FOR THE SEASONS

THE FALL OF MAN
In the fall, leaves fall
And make the man with the rake
Wish he had an axe.

COLD COMFORT
At first winter snow
Birds see no leaves on a tree
Just a place to rest.

IGNORANCE IS BLISS
To the birds of spring
That know nothing of the fall
The leaves are old friends.

ALZHEIMER IS NOT ALL BAD
Man in the summer
Soon forgets the awful fall
And bathes in cool shade.

ACORN MOON

The two were lying beneath the huge oak,
Its limbs stretching to embrace the autumn moon
The two moved closer together and as she filled his arms
He filled her and both were bound in each other's love.

And now each knew the serenity of passion spent.
And the huge oak no longer stretched out,
But seemed to hang down as if to enfold the lovers.

TIME ON MY HANDS

I watch the hands on the clock
As they tiptoe round and round.
I hear the tick and the tock.
Such a boring sound.

Tick-tock every second of the day
Is the master of every year.
No attention does anyone pay
Though it's there for all to hear.

There is no such thing as freedom
Only slaves to the clock
And the hands of the kingdom
With whips saying, "tick, tock"

I knew nothing of the race
Between me and the clock
Until the wrinkles on my face
Woke me with a shock.

From my deathbed I can see
The hands on the clock
As my breath goes out of me
I hear the tick, but not the tock.

Time To Die

It is Time who runs with no legs,
And has it all and never begs.
Whose outstretched hands reach across
Not to share but to boss.

His face is mouthless, but every day

He demands our labors anyway.
He sits and rules the earth
From the moment of our birth.
However
There is another king in the realm.
It is master Death at the helm.
He who has the upper hand
And is the terror of the land.

When all living things are dead
And no more blood is there to shed.
When there's nothing left to die
Does Death kneel and beg and cry?

The end will be the final crime,
Will it be Death who's killing time?
Or will Death go to hell?
Methinks only Time will tell.

TREE ENVY

Why do I envy the simple tree?
It has roots, while I am free.
I can move as I please.
It is subject to the breeze.

What I'll eat I can decide.
It eats only what roots provide.
It has no way to have the fun
In sinful ways as I have done.

And when it is fully-grown
From the seed that was sown
Someone will come around
And chop that big acorn down.

And quick as a wink
Before you can blink
It's fodder for the fireplace

Leaving ashes the only trace.

It burns for an hour, maybe two
Then it's over, completely through.
Why do I envy the simple tree?
You'd think it would envy me.

For my sins I'll burn in hell
Forever is what the preachers tell.
Forever is much too long for me.
Yes, I do envy the simple tree.

Death Equals All

The young marine is now at home,
Resting proudly in his tomb.
And, too, the soldier lies in peace,
His attentions now are all at ease.

At anchor, the sailor, from the storm
No longer needs his boilers warm.
The daring airman, from the sky
Has folded wings and cannot fly.

All these people drew their pay
For facing death everyday.
Sooner or later, they all knew,
This payday would come due.

The rich and poor, great and mere,
All at last must come to here.
Where all are equal, none the least.
None to famine while others feast.

While God has counted everyone,
Death also misses none.
Life, our prize, made so small
By one who waits to equal all.

THE COURAGE OF A COWARD

Bravery, to some, is all in the head
And to others, a hero must be dead
The difference in courage is in the deed,
Or so say they that have to bleed.

But no white knight would pick apart
The inner workings of a feeble heart
Until he has paid the coward's dues,
By walking a mile in timid shoes.

And once the lion has felt this shame,
Never again will he think the same.
He will think them meek no longer,
For he will know they are the stronger.

LOVING LISA

Smile, Mona, smile forever
Smile for Leo now or never.
I am sure when the task is done
Your smile will be number one

Leo, why must I be counted
Only after I am mounted?
The worth is yet unknown to me.
The purpose yet I cannot see.

Lisa, Lisa, such a smile
Will make this labor worth my while.
When we're dead you'll still be
Living, smiling eternally.

Leo, Leo, you're such a fool
If you believe in such a rule.
Smile you say, so smile I do.
I smile because of foolish you.

What care I when I'm gone
If my smile lives on and on?
In death I'm dead so in reality
What good to me is immortality?

Or . . . . MONEY MAD MONA
Smile, my Mona, smile for me.
And I will Paint just what I see.
Your smile will be to the world of art
The same as love to the human heart

And, my dear Mona, such a smile
Will make my labor well worthwhile
And when we're dead you'll still be
Living, smiling, eternally

Leo, Leo, save your breath
There is no life after death.
What care I when I'm gone
If my smile lives on and on?

What expenses will I have
As I rest in my grave?
Neither God nor Satan will decide
By my smile where I'll reside.

Smile you say, so smile I do,
But not, dear Leo, just for you.
The sweetest smile I can flash
Will cost you plenty cold hard cash

MITZI

Be not of little patience.
For all the work you've done
Starts as light from the moon,
A dim echo from the sun

Be not of little hope,
The sign of lunar light
Is all the proof you need
That the sun still shines at night

Be not too quick to turn the glass.
The sand will run out soon.
The sun will come at dawn
And put to bed the moon.

Be not of little faith
For all the seeds you've sown,
For with the coming of the sun
You'll see how all have grown.

Be not anyone but yourself
And you'll sway the heads of stone
And eternal as the Sun and Moon
You'll be not ever all alone.

Let they that enlighten, be called teachers,
And they that inspire, be called preachers.
And, leaders, those that show the way.
And who do all three, counselors, they.
Thanks Mitts

FIFTH ESTATE

As I speak someone else will write.
My hands are tied, both left and right.
I must tell the truth as I know it
Of the full true measure of any poet.

The pen is not where poems start
And neither is the fawning heart.
The hungry brain is the only way
The Pen and paper get to play.

The hunger is at once obsessive
Impulsive, compulsive, all possessive.
With a tortured soul and brain demented
The poet's love is hate tormented.

And if you saw me you would know
That what I write is really so.
For you see I'm in my hell,
A straight jacket and padded cell.

THE COST OF LIVING

If someone says "Follow me.
But only if you dare.
I'll show you all there is to see
And take you everywhere."

Hop aboard for the ride,
You may really get somewhere.
Be sure to choose an able guide,
For at the end, you are there.

And if he says the trip is free,
That he will foot the fare,
Glance back through history,
You know you'll pay your share.

CHAREE

There are thinkers, and dreamers, galore.
There are sitters and waiters by the score.
There are those who sit and wait for the dreams.
And those who think up all the schemes.

There are those that hate what they do.
And accept this as their due.
And those that do what they hate
Believing it given to them by fate.

You are a doer, and you will do
While thinkers and dreamers wait for you
To bring life to their dreams
And make success of their schemes.

Of all the thinkers, you are the best
As for the dreamers, you shame the rest.
But thinkers and dreamers only are for naught
You are also a doer and for that you'll be sought.

Dream of your future.
Think of how to get there
And do it.

THE GREEN SCREENED COMPUTER

I sat before the cyclops
And stared it in the eye
I watched its blood begin to flow,
That sickly greenish dye.

For months I probed its depths,
As I was taunted by
The magic that lay behind
That sickly greenish dye.

So ill and crazed I soon became,
My family said goodbye.
And I took note of nothing but,
That sickly greenish dye.

This monacled monster has no heart,
Shows no mercy, nor can it even cry.
No heart ever made could pump
That sickly greenish dye.

It sought to rule my very being,
But no one's slave am I.
It is I who am the master
Of that sickly greenish dye.

No, not today, nor ever again,
Would I gaze upon that hellish lie.
I knew I had to drain the blood . . .
That sickly greenish dye.

I pulled the plug and watched it fade
Into a puny colored dye.
A simple flick of switch had made
That sickly greenish die.

NO COUNT HEART

The computers are exact.
They only deal in fact.
But they can never feel.
They are only made of steel.

It is said they know, I know not how,
From my day of birth to here and now
My heartbeats they can count
So it's said, the right amount.

I do believe that any
Would fail and count too many.
They don't know the beat it skips
Every time I feel your lips.

DEFLATION HAIKU

The brown acorn fell
The great oak took no notice
There were so many.

FOOD BANK HAIKU

When the acorns fall
Squirrels always take notice
They thanked Katrina.

LAST LAUGH HAIKU

The proud oak tree stood,
Laughing at Katrina's winds
Loud but not for long.

STRONG HAIKU

The oak tree fell down
On the roof of the cabin
The wind laughed and left.

GREEN HAIKU

I write this haiku
On a tree that has been cut
And smashed into pulp.

THE SMOKING GUN

In the grave are many millions
Side by side with other billions.
The many millions are the jokers,
The rough and tough tobacco smokers.

Cut short in life and died in pain,
They tried to quit, but all in vain.
The best, I guess, that can be said
Is they got that for which they paid.

The bucket or the habit they could kick.
Their epitaphs here show their pick.
"The valiant soul herein lying
Tried to quit, still died trying."

THE GRAVITY OF MY MISTAKE

It has been my belief
That Mr. Time has been the thief
Who has caused my wrinkled skin
And woe, too, my double chin.

Caused my aching arches to fall
And made me not so tall.
My lady's breasts touch her knees
I gave him blame for all of these.

But, he was not the factor here
Although his sins are really near.
No, he is not one of depravity.
'Tis the one known as Mr. Gravity.

ROMAN TICS

Do as Romans, when in Rome,
And be yourself when at home
Hard to do by any man?
Not really, Italians can.

Pizza makers sit and mope,
Because there is a brand new pope.
They love John Paul, but sales are down,
Since Polish sausage came to town.

To Rome, directly, all roads lead.
For map or compass there is no need
The truth of this then lies in doubt
For once you're there, all roads lead out.

THE OTHER BROTHER

Am I my brother's keeper? Not I,
He is the apple of your eye.
You gave him the best,
And then let me have the rest.

He has only to tend his flock,
While I sow in soil as hard as rock.
He cares not where they wander
In my fields, here or over yonder.

My fields are always razed
After his sheep have grazed
He lets his sheep have feed
On crops I must use for seed.

Why must I work unfertile soil
Or from morn till night I must toil,
While he enjoys a life of ease
With sheep free from all disease.

All my labor done by hand
Leaves time for nothing but the land.
And for all this work you have no eyes,
And your ears are only for his lies.

You made us both what we are
And gave us each a different star.
So if I don't have what it takes
Why blame me for your mistakes?

My mom and dad are living proof
That even you can also goof.
So tell me not of great perfection
Until your deeds have stood correction.

Tell me, oh god, my brother's keeper,

Why do you ask that I dig deeper?
If you would give me at least my share,
I could then return what you think fair.

Tell me, oh god, my brother's keeper,
How high my hill, how much steeper?
I have given you the best of my lot,
And what to you is meager, to me is not.

And you ask, "where is your brother?"
Go great God, go ask another.
Or to quote you, if you don't mind,
Go God, "seek and you shall find."

TO SHARON LEE

Reach out for what you know you can't.
Be taller than you know you ain't.
Take the love you know is there
Give your love, its meant to share.

Fill your sleep with peaceful gladness
Lest you wake with troubled sadness.
Live your life, its all you have.
Taste the world, before the grave.

Bet your heart upon the dice
Have no fear to bet it twice.
Do what the world asks of you,
But do it only if you want it too.

So do your thing for Good or bad,
At four and thirty, you'll wish you had.
On the other hand, in late December
It won't matter, you won't remember.

TITI, CHAREE AND ME

Two heads are better than one,
Twice as good as having none.
So I took you for my wife,
Hoping for a better life.

The nights in May are very warm,
And does wonders for the lover's charm.
You lay beside me for a spell.
We became as one, then slept so well.

And from this union came anew
Then we're three no longer two.
Safety in numbers, I believe is true
So, stronger is three than just us two.

Near Beer
The boys came in for beer.
I told them that in here
The NA beer you buy
Will never get you high
The beer in here is near.

WHAT'S BEHIND THE BEAR

I went to hunt a bear.
A bear I knew was there.
And with my faithful gun
I shot him on the run
His behind is now bare with no hair to spare.

DAYDREAMS

I woke up with a fright
A nightmare not so slight
The fear was in my head
So I daydream in my bed
I no longer sleep at night.

JAMIE

A boy named Jamie Lynn
Grew right out of his skin
No matter what he ate
He could not lose the weight
That's the fix he was in.

PANCHITO

Pancho Juarez was so tall
To talk to him at all
From his feet it would take
All your change just to make
A short long distance call.

THIN SPIN

There was this kid so thin
Nothing but bones and skin
In fact he was so light
They used him for a kite
'Til a tailspin he went in.

Red Wine

His girl friend said, "No way."
She said this to Jose.
He was pouring the wine
He thought was Muscatine
But was just Vin Rose.

The Hairy Hare

The man who had no hair
Also had a hare.
The hare was just so big
He used it for a wig.
So he had a hare up there

Hairy Harry

Fuzzy Wuzzy was a bear
Hairy Harry was a hare
The reason Fuzzy had no hair
Was Harry robbed him of his share.
So Hairy Harry was not bare.

Speed

My life was flying past
The years were going fast.
When I was just a lad,
Time was all that I had.
Alas, that did not last.

Future Feature

I took my baby for a stroll
To ponder what our futures hold.
I did all of the talking.
She did none of the walking.
She's only eight months old.

TRAIN

The cow train was on a run
The cattle were all A-1
When the train caught on fire
As big as a New Year's pyre
The steaks were all well done.

BUS

The bus ran off the slope
The driver doing dope
It went down but he stayed high.
So did the driver die?
Nope!!!

THE PICK-UP

The boat went in the ditch
When it came off the hitch.
Said the driver of the truck,
"That is just my luck
A hitch with a glitch."

MEAT

A man by the name of Jim
Known to his friends as Slim
Wanting something to eat
Invented a treat
The Slim Jim was named for him.

THE LADY JEN

A great lady named Jen
Had a heart of gold within.
And years after she died
They found gold dust inside
The coffin where her bones had been.

BULL

Bill O'Dwyer the cattle buyer
Bought a bull full of ire.
He sent him to the vet
Came back minus a set
Bellowing an octave higher.

JADED

A lady flea by the name of Jade
When, at last, her eggs were laid
Was as happy as could be,
As much glee as could be for a flea.
Until she saw the can of "Raid".

NELLIE BELLE

There was a turtle named Nellie
Who was very proud of her belly.
They caught her on her back
And put her in their sack.
And now she's soup in a deli.

FARMER BROWN

Farmer Brown was with his goat
When a wave turned over his boat.
Farmer Brown was drowned
But his goat was found
The boat and the goat could float.

Saints Alive
A young lady by the name of Brewer
Was loved by all who knew her.
And when she died
The whole town cried
The world is one saint fewer

TEXAS TIME
There was a professor from Trenton,
By the name of Big Time Benton
He had the time, but he needed the space
When he heard of Texas, a faraway place,
Benton from Trenton moved to Denton.

STINKING SAILOR
The old sailor had a trunk
Full of beer under his bunk.
He never did see
The sights of the sea.
That trunk, under his bunk, kept him drunk as a skunk.

WRONG VECTOR HECTOR
The sailor's name was old Hector
Who always followed a wrong vector
When his ship the Anna Mae
Sank to the bottom one day
It was a Hector wrong vector that wrecked her.

DUCK DUCK
When the duck crossed the highway
"Quack, quack," he would say.
Which would stop every car
Except one went too far
On that day there was Pate'

PATRICK BADEAUX'S IGLOO

By

S. Kimo

As the ice cold wind blows on my face
I think about how lonely I am in this unpleasant place
I want to be home, this is not where I'm meant to be
I feel alone I want somebody with me.

As I wander blindly around this Arctic wasteland,
Trying to keep warm anyway I can
I think about wanting to see my family one last time
Yet just last week they weren't worth a dime.

It's a nice thing, being with someone who cares,
And out here there are dangerous things like crevices and
bears
I have made many mistakes in my life but this is the worst,
Yet the lesson learned is that family comes first.

If I ever get out of this frost-bitten night
I will go back to my family and make it all right.
I was not paying attention to where I was going
The crevice was invisible, due to the snowing.

But, before I could snap back to reality
I felt the overwhelming power of gravity
I will have to be strong
To right this wrong

WOODY AND THE DOGS

A.

The sun was coming up but John Elmwood couldn't see it. His cell had no window to the outside. It did have a small window with steel bars overlooking the corridor, but that was used more for looking in than looking out. The walls were padded.

"Ill have the last laugh on those yellow dogs," he was thinking to himself. They don't think I know how long I've been here in this cell, but I know. I know they have had me handcuffed here for three years. Three years as a stinking P.O.W."

"I'll make my escape this morning when they bring me to the shower. They take the handcuffs off when I shower. Only one guard at the shower and he doesn't have a gun. I can take him easy. Put his uniform on and just walk out of here. Once out of here I can find my way back to our lines." He was planning it confidently without knowing any details of who, what, where, or how.

Then he started thinking about how he got here. He didn't know that either. He remembered being on a patrol when the little yellow dogs came out of nowhere. "Over two dozen of them, firing and screaming, took me completely by surprise.

"I returned their fire and they started falling like rain in a hurricane. I got hit a bunch of times and kept on firing until I was standing alone on top of a pile of dead bodies. I had just enough strength to check 'em all out. All dead. I didn't give much for my chance of living either. I must have gone crazy because the last thing I remember was that if I were going to die I would make sure every one of those dogs would be dead before I hit the 'happy hunting grounds'. I put a bullet between the eyes of every one of those yellow suckers. I don't remember anything except pulling the trigger. With these two hands I personally wiped out two dozen."

When he stopped wondering about how he got here, he started remembering how he got there. "I didn't want to be in the army. I never killed anybody in my whole life. All my friends would go rabbit hunting and I would go bird watching. I wouldn't ride a horse because my dad told me I had to kick it to make it go. I had a choice; it was the army or prison. I chose the army and now I'm in a prison anyway. I must have been out of my mind to kill all of those people. I guess a person does strange things in time of war."

He heard noises outside his cell. They were coming to take him to the shower. He was ready. Then he heard them talking in English. They were trying to fool him again. They were trying to confuse him. Trying to make him tell secrets. Secrets he didn't know. Interrogations twice a day, in English. It didn't do any good because he didn't know any secrets. All he knew was his name, rank and service number and bits and pieces of his past life. He knew he wasn't a killer, but he was sure he knocked off over twenty Vietnamese in a matter of minutes. He tried to remember, but he couldn't.

"I'll remember as soon as I get out of here. I'll get help. The army has hospitals for people like me. All I have to do is get out of here and get back home," he thought. "If only our troops would have found me first; well I can't think about that now."

He heard the keys jingling in the corridor he was ready, "For whom the bells toll?" He tried to remember where he had heard that." It didn't matter; he was ready. "They toll for you this morning you Cong dogs." He said this out loud.

The key noise passed the door and he could no longer hear their conversation. That didn't matter either because he would only think it to be another trick.

"Hi, Bob. How's everything going this morning?" It was the head nurse, Bill, asking.

"Pretty good. Who are we going to start with this morning?' Bob asked.

"Mr. Elmwood. Doctor Lo Hin wants to see him first thing this morning. He has to go to San Francisco this afternoon. He has sent for John's mother and figures that if she can't bring him out of the fog, then nothing will." Bill was shaking his head to indicate the feeling of futility.

"He has been with us a month now and not even a sign of recognition. Doc has been trying to find out why he keeps his hands in his back pockets. Never takes them out except in the shower. When they found him in that waste disposal dump surrounded by a whole bunch of dead wild dogs, he was raving about killing every one of them. He was pretty badly bitten and was bleeding profusely. By the time they got him to the hospital he had gone into a coma and stayed that way for a week."

The phone rang and Bill answered it. "Okay, doctor, we'll have him ready. He turned to Bob and said, "The doc is coming down now so make sure everything is ready. He is bringing John's mother. I hope this works."

"This is John's mother. Open up and we'll see if this meeting will make any improvement." Doctor Lo Hin said.

When John saw his mother he started screaming, "Get her out of here! Get her out of here! She sold me out! It is all her fault! I remember now. She wouldn't give me the money to go to Canada. I hate her! Then he took his hands out of his back pockets and lunged at his mother's throat.

They subdued him and put him in a straight jacket. His mind snapped. He was now raving incoherently.

"I am sorry it didn't work out. I didn't know about the army. We didn't know anything until yesterday when the police missing person report came in." Doctor Lin Ho was apologizing to John's mother later in his office.

"We didn't even know he was missing until the army came to the house looking for him. That was only two days ago. I guess you know that the day they found him at the garbage dump was the same day he was to report to the army. I guess it was all too much for him. He was always such a gentle person; wouldn't swat a fly." John's mother said through sobs.

ANOTHER MONKEY'S PAW

A.

The place was called "The Coffee Cup" and it was primarily used for recovering alcoholics. There was a long table in the middle of the meeting room with sixteen chairs around it. There was a television at one end of the room, but hardly anybody watched it except for the World Series or the Super bowl. It was turned on, but the volume was turned down. A panel was talking about the drunks on Main Street and most certainly didn't know anything about drunks except that they smelled bad. What was so strange was that we used to think the same thing before we came into "Alcoholics Anonymous" and found out that most alcoholics don't live down there.

I turned away from the TV and joined a conversation that was going on in a corner of the room. My favorite person was talking. Judy made sense.

Judy had been one of the people that they were talking about on TV. She had been to the depths of degradation. She was hardheaded and had to go all the way to the bottom before asking for help. Her body, soul and mind had been the victim of alcoholism. Judy had committed every sin and had gone to any lengths to get a drink.

She had hit another drunk over the head with a bottle and almost killed him. The bottle only had enough for one more drink. They put her in jail for six months. That's when she came to "AA". That was about three years ago. She had been sober ever since. She was only thirty years old.

I remember this particular day well because she started aiming her remarks at me. At least that's what I thought because she was saying exactly what I needed to hear. She was like that; sharing her own experiences and knowledge. She was always dramatic and animated. I often thought about what a great schoolteacher she would have made.

Earlier that morning I had mentioned to Judy that I prayed to God for serenity. I had asked God to take my anxieties away and eliminate the confusion in my mind. I told her that prayers don't work because the only time I am not confused is when I am praying. "The whole world is screwed up," I told her. I asked her if I were doing something wrong.

That brought up the subject for that day's meeting. Everyone in the room had something to say on the subject, but nobody impressed me more than Judy.

In her Mississippi drawl Judy said, "When I first came to meetings I would ask God for patience. Every morning I asked. Twice more during the day I would pray. Every night I would plead with God to teach me patience. Lack of patience was my major character defect. All my life if I wanted something, I wanted it NOW. I didn't want to wait. I felt if I could learn patience I could easily handle the rest of my faults. I begged and pleaded to learn the patience I so desperately needed. I was about to give up on the whole concept of God. I was still short tempered. Nothing had changed. Prayers went unanswered.

"Then I went to the doctor because I was having headaches. They found a tumor on my brain. That was two years ago. Since then I have been in every major hospital in America. Hour after hour I have endured painful tests and operations. God had finally taught me patience. I have waited more in the last two years than I had in my entire previous life. So be careful of what you pray for because prayers are answered.

"I guess God knows that I now have learned enough patience because the doctors are sending me to California next week for a new experimental treatment. It is supposed to be the newest advance in cancer treatment. I prayed to God that this would be my last treatment. I think I have learned enough patience, enough for a lifetime.

"When you pray for something, make sure you really want it. It may be given to you in a way you might not like." She said and then got up to get a cup of coffee.

That was the last time I saw Judy. She went to California for her great treatment. The treatment failed. She died in the recovery room. Her prayers were answered. That was her last treatment.

I don't pray anymore.

Editor's note: If you've read "Cajun Conspiracy" you know A.'s grandfather was the biggest liar in the world. A. makes his grandfather look more truthful than George Washington in comparison. Don't believe a word of this story. He was probably drunk on Main St. when he wrote it.

"Bless you Boys"

God bless America

Please pray for our troops.

A LETTER TO PATRICK

Dear Patrick,

I am sorry that I won't be home for your sixth birthday. I am in Africa now, but I am sending you a polar bear skin from Alaska that has an unbelievable story. If I weren't there to see it with my own eyes I wouldn't believe it myself.

After my first pilot, One Eye, crashed into a mountain and died they sent me another pilot named Sam. He doesn't want me to tell his last name because it would be too embarrassing. He said that it happened to him before a long time ago aboard a boat. (I personally don't believe him, but if it happened this time I guess it could have happened before.)

It happened on our way out after we closed down our Arctic Circle radar camp. The helicopter lost power and went down. It took Sam so long to fix it that he froze to death. He was a solid block of ice. I didn't have a shovel to bury him, but I did have an axe so I cut down a pine tree and lit a fire and threw him in it. I was going to cremate him.

I eventually found the trouble with the engine; it had lost a cotter pin. I replaced it with one of the bear claws from the bearskin and was about to take off when I saw Sam running to the chopper. He was naked as the day he was born because the fire had burned off all his clothes. He got in the chopper and put on the bearskin. He said that was the second time he had been warm since he left some place in Tennessee.

When we arrived at the airport and he got out the security guard started shooting at him. I jumped out of the chopper waving and shouting to the guard that it wasn't a bear, but only Sam. I left him at the hospital; he said he was in good hands because he had Allstate insurance.

I arrived in Africa yesterday and am on the way to the head of the Nile. I guess your mama told you that your uncle is up there trying to find a cure for the tsetse fly sleeping sickness. He was supposed to have found the cure and was waiting for the Nobel Prize. The word I got just before heading up there was that he injected himself with his serum and all it did was paralyze the eyelids so they don't close. He hadn't slept in two weeks. They think his eyeballs have shrunk. I don't think he is going to get the Nobel Prize. He'll be lucky if he ever gets to sleep again.

I had to interrupt writing this letter because one of the scouts came in and said that a six—foot alligator ate his brother. I tried to tell him that alligators only have four feet, but I guess it got lost in the translation. Anyway I guess the number of teeth an alligator has is more important than how many feet it has.

I have to get to sleep now. I will write more tomorrow.

It is in the afternoon now and it has been an awesome day. We ran into a man—eating lion and our guide didn't want to take any chances so he sent his sister out to kill it. I'll bring you that skin when I come home.

Then we saw a herd of Arbez. They were thought to be extinct. They look like a black horse with white stripes and are sometimes confused with a Zebra that is white with black stripes. That's probably why they were thought to be extinct.

We should be at the head of the Nile tomorrow, but our guide took a wrong turn. We hired him because his resume' said "headhunter". He showed up with a bunch of shrunken heads hanging from his belt. We hired him anyway because it was too late to find somebody else.

I will only be able to stay here for a few days because I just received a coded message from the pentagon. They want me to go somewhere. I'll tell you about it in my next letter. I don't know where I'll be going because the guy on the drums can't spell worth a darn. They want me to investigate the murder of the "Brown Octopus". He is the world's most top-secret spy. He was so top secret that he didn't even know that he was the "Brown Octopus". Probably why he got killed.

Happy Birthday, I hope you will enjoy the bearskin.

Love,
Grandpa Dick

Dear Grandpa,

Thanks for the bearskin. Mamma put in front of the fireplace.

Grandma says you are a secret spy. I don't understand if you are a secret spy how does she know about it. She told me so your secret isn't much of a secret. Be careful. You'll have to have a long talk with Grandma. I won't tell anybody your secret. I told Grandma that I want to be a secret spy just like you when I grow up. I won't tell anybody but you. I have to go to school now, but I will write more tomorrow.

Love, Patrick

That was a long time ago. Patrick just joined the Navy. He is not a secret spy. (If he is he didn't tell me.)

MAKE NO MISTAKE

You hit us hard that day
And brought us to our knees.
But MNM, that's the way
We send to God our pleas.

You hit us hard that day.
Our buildings came apart
But, MNM, I say.
We're one united heart.

You hit us hard that day.
You brought panic doubt and fear.
But MNM, our dismay
Has reached our great God's ear.
You hit us hard that day,
You ugly fleas were biting.
But MNM, this dog won't stay
Scratching without fighting.

You hit us hard that day
And crawled back in your hole.
But MNM, you worms will pay.
When we send, to hell, your soul.

You hit us hard that day
And shook the dog awake.
MNM, its time for you to pray.
You've made your big mistake
G.W.'s PROMISE